MODIFIED RAPTURE
Comedy in W. S. Gilbert's Savoy Operas

VICTORIAN LITERATURE AND CULTURE SERIES

Karen Chase, Jerome J. McGann, *and* Herbert Tucker,

General Editors

Daniel Albright
 Tennyson: The Muses' Tug-of-War

David G. Riede
 Matthew Arnold and the Betrayal of Language

Anthony Winner
 Culture and Irony: Studies in Joseph Conrad's Major Novels

James Richardson
 *Vanishing Lives: Style and Self in Tennyson, D. G. Rossetti,
 Swinburne, and Yeats*

Jerome J. McGann, Editor
 Victorian Connections

Anthony Harrison
 Victorian Poets and Romantic Poems: Intertextuality and Ideology

E. Warwick Slinn
 The Discourse of Self in Victorian Poetry

Linda K. Hughes and Michael Lund
 The Victorian Serial

Anna Leonowens
 The Romance of the Harem
 Edited with an Introduction by Susan Morgan

Alan Fischler
 "Modified Rapture": Comedy in W. S. Gilbert's Savoy Operas

Barbara Timm Gates, Editor
 Journal of Emily Shore, with a new Introduction by the Editor

MODIFIED RAPTURE

Comedy in
W. S. Gilbert's Savoy Operas

by

Alan Fischler

UNIVERSITY PRESS OF VIRGINIA

Charlottesville and London

To Stan and Miriam Fischler

THE UNIVERSITY PRESS OF VIRGINIA
Copyright © 1991 by the Rector and Visitors
of the University of Virginia

First published 1991

Library of Congress Cataloging-in-Publication Data

Fischler, Alan.
  "Modified rapture" : comedy in W.S. Gilbert's Savoy operas / by
Alan Fischler.
    p.   cm.—(Victorian literature and culture series)
  Includes index.
   ISBN 0-8139-1334-9
   1. Gilbert, W. S. (William Schwenck), 1836–1911—Criticism and
interpretation.   2. Comedy.   3. Opera.   I. Title.   II. Series.
PR4714.F57   1991
822'.8—dc20   91–6832
                                                                    CIP

Printed in the United States of America

Contents

Preface

THOUGH MY INTENSIVE CONSIDERATION OF W. S. Gilbert's comedy begins with *H.M.S. Pinafore,* Gilbert's career did not. My decision to focus on a relatively small portion of his dramatic canon requires explanation.

Gilbert's first play, *Uncle Baby,* was produced in 1863, fifteen years before *Pinafore.* In 1866, with the burlesque *Dulcamara,* his work as a dramatist began in earnest. Between then and the premiere of *Pinafore,* Gilbert wrote, adapted, translated, or contributed to at least forty-nine comedies, extravaganzas, burlesques, pantomimes, farces, dramas, and comic operas. Included in this total are his first three librettos to music by Arthur Sullivan: *Thespis* (1871), *Trial By Jury* (1875), and *The Sorcerer* (1877).

Gilbert had some notable hits during this period: *Pygmalion and Galatea* (1871), for instance, eventually earned its author £40,000. But the author had just as many notable failures: *Thespis,* the first Gilbert and Sullivan opera, opened just seventeen days after *Pygmalion and Galatea* but ran only sixty-four performances and was never revived. Nor did Gilbert achieve any consistent record of success to match the string that Tom Robertson ran from 1865 to 1870 at the Prince of Wales's Theatre; nor did he have any single success of the magnitude of H. J. Byron's *Our Boys,* which ran for an incredible 1,362 performances from 1875 to 1879. Before *Pinafore,* in short, Gilbert may have begun to establish himself in the theater, but he had done no more than many of his contemporaries to attract Victorian audiences to stage comedy.

Moreover, before *Pinafore,* we find no evidence that the Gilbert and Sullivan partnership was regarded, by either the public or the partners themselves, as a permanent arrangement. Indeed, the librettist had more frequently collaborated with composer Frederic Clay and was continuing to do so as late as 1876. Nor could the 175 performances achieved by *The Sorcerer* in 1877–78 have constituted an especially gratifying success for either partner: Gilbert and Clay, after all, had done twice as well with *Ages Ago* (1869), while Sullivan and F. C. Burnand had seen their *Cox and Box* begin a run of 300 performances in the same year. Thus, had *Pinafore* met with the same polite but passionless reception that had greeted their first three operas, Gilbert and Sullivan might well have gone their separate ways.

But, as even the most casual student of the Savoy operas knows, the reception accorded *Pinafore* was anything but passionless. Not only did it run 700 performances, but it spawned a rival production in London and a mania in the United States. What was past was scarcely even prologue to this.

The present study contends that *Pinafore* represents the turning point not only in Gilbert's theatrical fortunes but, more importantly, in his comic dramaturgy. In Chapter 1 I will argue that no Victorian dramatist of the pre-*Pinafore* era produced comedy that was substantially congenial to the middle class, who constituted the most potentially lucrative but persistently aloof segment of the theatrical market. Gilbert himself was no exception to this rule, even in his early work with Sullivan. Chapter 1 will attempt to show that earlier nineteenth-century plays in general, and the first three Gilbert and Sullivan operas in particular, followed the subversively anti-legal pattern that Shakespeare and his successors had established as traditional on the English comedic stage.

But my chief concern is with the causes of Gilbert's eventual great success, and I will therefore concentrate on the later operas. I will argue that the dramaturgy born in *Pinafore* and propagated by the subsequent Savoy librettos differed markedly from the work that Gilbert and others had previously done for the Victorian theater. Law and authority, with which the bourgeoisie had come to identify their interests, lost the malignity which comedy had traditionally ascribed to them and emerged as the prime salvational forces of Gilbert's tales; at the same time, the unblinkingly theistic assumptions of earlier nineteenth-century drama, which must have grated unpleasantly against post-Darwinian religious anxieties, were edited out. Indeed, in Gilbert's mature work, human law was established as a substitute for Providence, as it not only assumed the function of disentangling plot difficulties but also meted out rewards and punishments in infallible accord with the duty-based morality that the middle class professed to hold dear. That the implementation of this new approach and the upsurge in box-office business—an upsurge enabled in no small part by middle-class patronage—happened at the same time seems to me no coincidence.

In Chapter 2, then, I will attempt to analyze both this new approach to comedy and its peculiar appeal to bourgeois prejudices. The focus will be on the "high Savoy operas"—those written during the period of Gilbert's greatest popularity, when his distinctive dramaturgy was most fully developed. These include: *H.M.S. Pinafore* (1878), *The Pirates of Penzance* (1880), *Patience* (1881), *Iolanthe* (1882), *Princess Ida* (1884), *The Mikado* (1885), *Ruddigore* (1887), *The Yeomen of the Guard* (1888), and *The Gondoliers* (1889). I will also draw upon the last two Savoy operas, *Utopia (Limited)* (1893) and *The Grand Duke* (1896), for examples of Gilbert's mature approach to comedy; at the same time, though, I will attempt in Chapter 3 to explain why these two pieces met with considerably less public favor than most of their nine predecessors.

My text for the Savoy operas is *The First Night Gilbert and Sullivan* (first published in 1958 and reissued in a 1975 Centennial Edition), which is the work of the late Reginald Allen, the foremost bibliographical scholar on matters Gilbertian. In addition to its authoritative librettos, Allen's edition provides excerpts from reviews of the premieres and records the changes that Gilbert made once critics and audiences had voiced their opinions on the early performances of each piece. As my study is concerned with the dramatist's efforts to season his work to the tastes of the public, this edition has been of enormous value to me.

Finally, I should note that I have taken the liberty of regularizing punctuation and capitalization (especially of play titles) within some quotations from my sources.

Acknowledgments

I hope that my text and my notes have adequately acknowledged my enormous indebtedness to those scholars whose work has enabled and enriched my own. On a more personal note, I wish to thank the following people, each of whom has made a unique and invaluable contribution to my work: My friend, Dr. Harold Kanthor, generously gave me free access to his splendid private collection of materials by and about Gilbert, and otherwise facilitated my research from the start to the finish of this project. Professors Richard Gollin and Jarold Ramsey, of the University of Rochester, encouraged me and helped me complete my first draft. Their criticism guided me toward reshaping it into a more coherent argument. My typist, Betsy Haines, responded with unfailing good humor and expedition to both reasonable and unreasonable demands. My ex-wife, Pat Bonino, provided solace and support through most of the years that I worked on this project. Ms. Nancy Essig, the staff of the University Press of Virginia, and the editors of the Victorian Literature and Culture Series, offered suggestions for revisions that have strengthened my book in more ways than I can possibly credit. My father, Stanley Fischler, first taught me to appreciate Gilbert. To him and to my mother, Miriam, this work is, with much love, dedicated.

A Faculty Research Grant from the Rochester Institute of Technology's College of Liberal Arts helped to defray some of the expenses involved in revising my manuscript. Two more grants from the Le Moyne College Research and Development Committee provided funds for a subsequent round of revisions, and this same committee's approval of a course-load reduction provided the time to do the actual work. My thanks for all.

MODIFIED RAPTURE
Comedy in W. S. Gilbert's Savoy Operas

I

Introduction

A Knight in the Theater

IN THE CENTURY between the end of Sheridan's playwriting career and the beginning of Shaw's, W. S. Gilbert stands without close rival as the most successful and significant of all British dramatists. His popularity became international when *H.M.S. Pinafore* (1878) was imported by the United States, where it was "simultaneously performed in over one hundred theatres of America"[1] at the same time it was achieving an incredible run of 700 performances in London. In 1881, a new theater, the Savoy, was built expressly to serve "as a permanent home for the Gilbert and Sullivan Operas," and its opening was attended by a "brilliant audience . . . the Prince and Princess of Wales heading the list."[2] In 1884, in a poll conducted by *Truth* to determine the British public's favorite playwright, Gilbert surprisingly placed only third;[3] however, the results are put into perspective when one considers that H. J. Byron and Tom Robertson, who finished ahead of him, were, respectively, at and past the end of their careers, while Gilbert still had before him such successes as *The Mikado, The Yeomen of the Guard,* and *The Gondoliers.* Indeed, by 1888 he could declare to Sullivan, with justifiable pride, "We have the best theatre, the best company, the best composer, and (though I say it) the best librettist in England working together—we are world-known, and as much an institution as Westminster Abbey."[4] Two years later, Gilbert's wealth had become such that he was able to assume the role of country squire through the purchase of Grim's Dyke, a large house to the north of London, filled with art, antiques, and other solid evidence of success. But only in 1911, when the dramatist's will was probated, did it become fully apparent how rich the theater had made him. In 1862, the year before his first play was produced, Gilbert had regarded the receipt of a £300 inheritance as "the happiest day of my life" because it enabled him to quit a civil service job that he detested;[5] forty-nine years later, just after his final play had been staged, his estate was valued at £112,000.[6]

Of course, we are not surprised to learn that the librettist of the most popular operas ever written in English became a rich man, but the author himself and his mid-nineteenth century contemporaries must have been quite surprised. For a young man just beginning his literary career in the sixties had little reason to dream that a life spent writing for the stage would be crowned by wealth. The bourgeoisie, who had been enthusiastic patrons of the playhouses through most of the 1700s, had been "crowded out" in the course of the urbanization that accompanied the Industrial Revolution. By the early nineteenth century, the English theater, for the most part, had become the preserve of the poor working class, with prices—and financial rewards for authors—scaled down accordingly. In 1826, Prince Pückler-Muskau had visited London and reported that "The most striking thing to a foreigner in English theatres is the unheard-of coarseness and brutality of the audiences. The consequence is that the higher and more civilized classes go only to the Italian operas, and very rarely visit their national theatre." This is not to say that certain playhouses did not sporadically surface as islands of respectability or that certain individual pieces did not capture the bourgeois fancy: indeed, the appeal of a popular performer or the splendor of a particular production often resulted in a hit that even polite society deigned to attend. But, for all these scattered exceptions, the fundamentally hostile disposition of the respectable middle class toward the stage remains clear. Allardyce Nicoll confirms the "cringing disapproval" with which "bourgeois opinion regarded" the early nineteenth-century theater.[7]

Moreover, by Gilbert's time, they had made a half-century's habit of holding aloof from the playhouses and were thus harder than ever to lure. In a 1927 article entitled "When Gilbert and Sullivan Began," Charles E. Grigsby recalled that, in his mid-Victorian boyhood, "Theatres in those days were beyond our reach. Bus and tram services were bad and there was no catering for the suburbs as we have today. Still another obstacle to theatre-going was the stern, religious middle-class conscience that had no love for the theatre or regarded it, together with the dancing hall, as an ante room to Hell." Indeed, there were "many thousands of serious families who were convinced that the playhouse was the favorite resort of the devil."[8]

But why should the bourgeoisie's hostility toward the theater have so decisively diminished its profitability? They did not, to be sure, constitute the largest pool of potential theatergoers; an 1867 study devoted to "calculating the size of the various British classes" found that "over three-quarters—seventy-seven percent—of the 24.1 million inhabitants of Britain belonged to the 'manual labour class.'" But nineteenth-century theatrical managers had long since discovered how little money there was to be made from playhouses run exclusively for the proletariat, however numerous they may have been. This was especially true at the two patent houses, the enormous size of which enhanced the opportunity for both profit and loss:

> From the financial viewpoint alone, Drury Lane and Covent Garden suffered as badly before the abolition of their monopoly on the legitimate drama in 1843 as after it. . . . In the 1820s and 1830s Elliston, Price, Lee, Polhill, Bunn, and Hammond tried to make a success of management but were driven into retreat and backruptcy. Macready's management of 1841–43 also proved a financial failure. . . . During a similar period Covent Garden had as many managers—Charles Kemble, Laporte, Bunn, Osbaldiston, Macready, Vestris—and fared as badly as its rival. . . . Drury Lane did not become a successful financial venture until after Augustus Harris took it over in 1879. Covent Garden never recovered, and became an opera house in 1847.

Nor was the financial plague confined to these two houses: "Their competitors, the minor theatres, where before 1843 only the 'illegitimate' drama containing songs and music could be staged, did not do much better. Theatrical hard times prevailed almost everywhere in the first half of the century, and the long-awaited abolition of the patent monopoly in 1843 brought relief to neither major nor minor theatres." Analysis suggests the crucial role that the middle-class boycott played in sustaining this situation: in an age in which

"Typical audiences were composed mainly of lower-class citizens with a sprinkling of representatives from the gayer and more libertine section of the aristocracy,"[9] the latter were not numerous enough to fill the expensive box seats, and the former were not rich enough to buy any other than the cheap seats in the pit and the gallery.

Inevitably, the illnesses of the nineteenth-century theater were visited upon its authors. In 1832, four years before Gilbert's birth, Douglas Jerrold had bitterly complained:

> *Were we asked what profession promised with the greatest show of success, to form a practical philosopher, we should on the instant make reply, "The calling of an English dramatist." . . . The daily lessons set for him to con are decked with that "consummate flavour" of wisdom, patience; they preach to him meekness under indigence; continual labour with scanty and uncertain reward; quiescence under open spoilation; satisfaction to see others garner the harvest he has sown; with at least the glorious certainty of that noble indigence lauded by philosophers and practised by the saints—poverty, stark-naked poverty, with grey hairs; an old age exulting in its forlornness!*

In 1856, just seven years before the start of Gilbert's playwriting career, the status of this calling had not improved much: an article from *Blackwood's Magazine* of that year "cites cases of the audience at a new play calling before the curtain for its commendation, not the actor, certainly not the author, but the scenic artist." In a theater in which uneducated tastes had induced "the complete subordination of comedy to spectacle,"[10] a comic dramatist was a person of no particular importance. As far as he could know when he saw his *Uncle Baby* mounted in 1863, Gilbert was embarking upon a voyage bound for no more certain destination than obscurity.

And yet, forty-four years later, we find this same Gilbert being knighted by Edward VII, while the *Times* lauded him as one "whose works have become classical and the object of such fervent affection as classics seldom enjoy." Clearly, in the intervening decades, dramatic changes had occurred in respectable society's perception of the theater and in the dignity accorded to its playwrights.

And, just as clearly, Gilbert was recognized as having been at the forefront of this change, for he could proudly reflect after receiving his knighthood that he was, to date, "the only dramatic author upon whom, *qua* dramatic author, it has ever been conferred."[11]

To the same extent that Gilbert surpassed earlier nineteenth-century dramatists in fame, so he did in fortune. In contrast to Gilbert and his £112,000 estate stands Frederick Reynolds, in his prime during the early years of the century, who "after a career of nearly sixty years, owned to earning £19,000, no dazzling fortune, but in his words: 'a sum unequalled in the history of dramatic writing.'"[12] In the same era, George Colman the Younger, preeminent among playwrights, typically received only £550 for a five-act comedy.[13] In the decades following, matters became still worse: by the fifties, "the ordinary author could not look for more than a maximum of about £50 per act"[14]—especially when managers could so easily commission translations of ready-made and Paris-proven French comedies for only £25 each.[15] Gilbert himself sold his second play for only £30 in 1866. In stark contrast, just forty years later he was able to boast that *Ruddigore*—an 1887 opera widely considered to be a failure—had, "with the sale of the libretto, put £7,000 into my pocket."[16]

Even in the era after the sixties, when the establishment of the modern royalty system and the "long run" began to enhance the returns that authors realized from popular pieces, Gilbert's success stands out. Tom Robertson, one of the first beneficiaries of both these changes, was "by the end of his unhappily brief life" in 1871 only "earning £4,000 a year";[17] Gilbert, on the other hand, saw his annual income rise as high as £20,000[18] and claimed in 1908 to be receiving £3,000 a year in book royalties on the Savoy librettos alone.[19] Moreover, during the period of his greatest triumphs—from the opening of *Pinafore* in 1878 through the closing of *The Gondoliers* in 1891—Gilbert achieved his wealth while averaging about one new play a year; Robertson, in contrast, produced six new plays in 1869, his last full year of activity before his health began seriously to fail.

The extent of Gilbert's financial achievement becomes even more remarkable when considered against the economic background of his age. For "the years between 1873 and 1896" were an era of "spectacular . . . deflation" in Great Britain, which "are known to economic historians, who have discussed them more eagerly than any other phase of nineteenth-century business conjecture, as the 'Great Depression.' . . . Prices, profits and rates of interest fell or stayed puzzlingly low. A few feverish little booms did not really halt this long and frustrating descent, which was not reversed until the middle 1890s."[20] Yet these were the years in which all but one of the Gilbert and Sullivan operas were written and in which Gilbert became affluent. We can only wonder how much money he might have made in a time of prosperity.

How then, with the economic odds stacked against him and attitudes toward dramatists rising barely above contempt, could any nineteenth-century author of stage plays have achieved a career blessed by riches and honors? The answer consists in the same crucial variable that had, by its absence, rendered Gilbert's predecessors impoverished: the patronage of the middle class, whose impact upon the arts, politics, and all other aspects of English life became even more decisive in the century's second half. Though still a relatively small percentage of the population, their absolute magnitude was growing: "The widest definition of the middle class or those who aspired to imitate them was that of keeping domestic servants. Their numbers . . . increased very substantially from 900,000 in 1851 to 1.4 million in 1871."[21] At the same time, the bourgeois audience was also growing more accessible, as the mid-century development of both the railway and the omnibus made it increasingly practical for those who lived in the suburbs to attend the theater on a regular basis.[22] The only remaining problem was to persuade them to do so.

The process actually began almost simultaneously with the bourgeois boom. In the early fifties, Charles Kean, with Dion Boucicault as his house playwright, enjoyed considerable success as manager at the Princess's Theatre, especially after Queen Victoria herself showed the way to respectable society by coming five times to Boucicault's *The Corsican Brothers*.[23] In 1856, Priscilla and Thomas German Reed, determined to seduce those respectable citizens who would never have entered a playhouse, opened an establishment which they carefully called not a "theater" but rather the "Gallery of Illustration," at which they presented "entertainments"—never "plays"—with "splendid success" into the seventies.[24] Another theatrical couple, Squire and Marie Bancroft, combined their efforts with Tom Robertson's to succeed in "coaxing back polite society" into their magnificently refurbished Prince of Wales's Theatre in the late sixties.[25]

Still, the success that both the Reeds and the Bancrofts aimed at, and achieved, was relatively modest: the Gallery of Illustration could hold just 500 patrons, and the Prince of Wales's about the same number. But Richard D'Oyly Carte, the producer of the last thirteen of the fourteen Gilbert and Sullivan operas, dreamed not just of profits but of fortune, and, when he saw *H.M.S. Pinafore* consistently packing the 862-seat Opera Comique, determined to build a new theater which would enable his authors to work their alchemy on a larger scale. The Savoy, opened in 1881 with a capacity of about 1,300,[26] was half again as large as the old theater and accordingly more costly to operate and maintain. Gilbert, indeed, was less than confident about the financial wisdom of this move, complaining to Carte that "If we play for a year to an average of £120 nightly receipts, we make at the Opera Comique £9,000 a year—and we lose at the Savoy £3,000 a year. You will see at once that this is simple ruination."[27] But there was enormous potential for profit as well as ruin, for the Savoy had enough seats, and high enough prices, that a full house would yield about £270—just £100 less than the average nightly takings of the 3,060-seat Drury Lane at its most lucrative point in the earlier nineteenth century.[28] And the frequency with which Gilbert and Sullivan succeeded in adequately filling their new theater—especially its more expensive sections—is attested to by the wealth not only of the librettist but also of the manager who had sense enough to build it: when he died in 1901, Carte left behind an estate of £241,000, more than twice as much as Gilbert's.[29]

That the occupants of the stalls, boxes, and dress circle of the Savoy Theatre were drawn from the very best society has been well-documented.[30] Of course, the middle-class presence in these audiences is difficult to quantify, but we can have little doubt that this presence increased in direct proportion to the growth of the Gilbert and Sullivan partnership's respectability. Two contrasting anecdotes illustrate the rapidity and extent of this growth. When George Grossmith, a successful entertainer at chaste recitals patronized by staid churchgoers, was invited in 1877 to play the title role in *The Sorcerer*, "his chief fear, as confided to D'Oyly Carte, was that his appearance on the stage would ruin forever his chances for engagements by the Young Men's Christian Association and other such religious organizations." But, just nineteen years later, when the Hungarian countess Ilka von Palmay was asked to take the soprano lead in *The Grand Duke*, she considered it not just a professional but a social opportunity. Her memoirs recall:

> *The Savoy Theatre was at that time the premier stage in England after Covent Garden, and I dare say the most high-class. So, for example, no lady had set foot on the boards of this theatre either in stockinet or in male costume, for it was considered not at all comme il faut. French operettas in particular did not achieve performance here because of their obscenity. . . . On pain of instant dismissal all obscene talk and any such act was forbidden in every room of the house. These articles had for years always been followed so conscientiously and strictly that a high-class mode of thinking and living was instilled into the flesh and blood of everyone belonging to the Savoy Theatre without exception down to the most modest member of the chorus. The members of the company are so placed with their salaries that they are able to cover the necessities of life handsomely. So belonging to the Savoy Theatre in itself bestows a certain social status and secures esteem in the best circles.[31]*

Von Palmay evidently did not know that Gilbert and Sullivan had begun their partnership with a piece in which two of the star attractions were Nelly Farren's legs, displayed in the tights she donned to play the male role of Mercury in 1871's *Thespis;* nor was she likely to have known that *Trial By Jury*, the second Gilbert and Sullivan opera, had originally been produced as an afterpiece to Offenbach's *La Périchole*. But the countess's ignorance is, itself, evidence of the collaborators' success in expunging their youthful indiscretions from the public memory and reforming themselves into the bespoke entertainers of the bourgeoisie.

Still, if respectability drew these previously recalcitrant customers to the Opera Comique and the Savoy, the question remains of how the Gilbert and Sullivan operas attained it. The answer, I believe, is implicit in the reasons that the works of their predecessors—and, for that matter, the early efforts of Gilbert and Sullivan themselves—failed to do so.

"Hollow Is the Laughter Free": Comedy and the Victorian Middle Class

The nineteenth-century English theater was almost wholly devoted to comedy. Original tragedies were being written by such authors as Joanna Baillie, James Sheridan Knowles, and Thomas Noon Talfourd—whose names became even more rapidly buried in obscurity than those of their less serious contemporaries—and audiences were offered perennial revivals of tragedies by Shakespeare, Otway, and others. Nevertheless, at both the major and the minor houses, the bill for any given evening and the repertoire for any given season were more likely to be stuffed with farces, burlesques, extravaganzas and, at Christmas, pantomimes.

Even melodrama, the most popular and most vital of all Victorian stage genres, was essentially comedic. Boucicault, perhaps the century's foremost melodramatist, confessed this much in comparing himself with Robertson, the leading author of "pure" comedy. "The public pretend they want pure comedy," he wrote to Marie Bancroft in 1868; "that is not so. What they want is domestic drama treated with broad comedy character. A sentimental, pathetic play, comically rendered, such as *Ours, Caste, Colleen Bawn, Arrah-na-Pogue*. Robertson differs from me not fundamentally, but scenically; his action takes place in lodgings and drawing-rooms— mine has a more romantic scope."[32] Generally, of course, the proportions of sentiment and pathos were higher in melodrama, and the result was a predominant seriousness of tone. But the pity aroused by these plays was unaccompanied by terror, for one of the genre's outstanding features was the comforting assertion that a beneficent Providence superintends the affairs of humanity, punishing the wicked and protecting the good. Consequently, it failed to fulfill the Aristotelian definition of tragedy; conversely, if comedy is broadly conceived to encompass all drama that assigns happy fates to most of its sympathetic characters and arranges the proper couplings between its eligible young people, it becomes clear how Victorian melodrama ought to be categorized.

It was comedy, then, that the middle class was rejecting in its boycott of the theater.[33] The all-purpose charge of "indecency" was invoked to explain their attitude, but a reading of the period's plays does not sustain it: as Nicoll remarks, "It is one of the jests of literature that, in this age of such decorous and sentimentally moral dramas, a reviewer could declare that 'now it is almost dangerous to take a young person to a playhouse.'" Such unthinking attacks suggest an alienation so advanced that it had become unwilling even to account credibly for itself. And its causes were, indeed, deeply rooted, as Bulwer-Lytton recognized in 1841:

> *In the old comedy there is a laugh at everything most serious. But in that day . . . the fashion in real life ran in the same direction. In Shakespeare the dishonour of a husband is the material for revenge and tragedy; in Congreve and Wycherley it is the most fruitful food for ridicule and burlesque. But these last writers as artists have their excuse; they are not writing for the pulpit or the academy, but for the stage, and they must embody the manners and morals that they observe around them. It is precisely because the present age is more thoughtful, that Comedy, in its reflection of the age, must be more faithful to the chequered diversities of existence and go direct to its end through humours to truth, no matter whether its path lie through smiles or tears.*

Christopher Herbert, from a more chronologically detached vantage, makes a similar point. Arguing his thesis that "Comedy in mid-Victorian England was an anachronistic literary type, deeply foreign to contemporary taste and sensibility, and no writer could have practiced it with impunity," he explains that "Victorian readers were necessarily alienated from traditional stage comedy . . . by its deeply ingrained quality of stylization and artificiality, which could not fail to offend a middle-class public whose cardinal principle for evaluating literary works was that of direct, faithful representation of reality, a principle expressing a Wordsworthian tradition based on ideals of naturalness, sincerity, and deep feeling—and that left little room for the preposterous artificialities of traditional comedy."[34] In short, the problem confronting dramatists was not a superficial one of decorum nor even tone: it was the more fundamental problem of reconciling comedy with the philosophical spirit of the Victorian age.

Northrop Frye distills the essence of this spirit:

> *Ordinary social consciousness usually begins in a sense of antithesis between what the ego wants and what society will allow it to have. Hence temporal authority comes to the individual first of all in the form of an external compulsion. In this stage, freedom is identified with the ego's side of the antithesis. But education, and more particularly education of the reason, introduces us to a form of necessity or compulsion which is not opposed to freedom but seems rather to be another aspect of it. To assent to the truth of a geometrical demonstration is psychologically a contrast to assenting to the will of a social superior. Hence reason can do what faith, hope and even love by themselves cannot do: present us with the model or pattern of an authority which appeals to the mind rather than to the body, which compels but does not enforce. Such authority confers dignity on the person who accepts it.*

Of course, Victorian thinkers differed widely from one another in identifying the source of that authority which the ego ennobles itself by obeying: Newman found it in the Church, Carlyle in the leadership of heroes, Arnold in the cumulative wisdom of culture, and Mill in the will of the majority as shaped by free and full debate. But they agreed that such a source existed and that its locus was external to the individual will. In Carlyle's thunderous formulation of this axiom of the age, "*Thou shalt* was from of old the condition of man's being, and his weal and blessedness was in obeying that. Woe for him when, were it on the hest of the clearest necessity, rebellion, disloyal isolation, and mere *I will,* becomes his rule!"[35]

The most notable dissenters from this creed were the early and mid-century middle classes. Still struggling to rise on the economic and social scales, they were attracted by the ideas of Utilitarianism, which gave them a philosophical cloak to throw over their naked pursuit of self-interest. The Liberal Party, with its agenda of voluntaryism in religion, free trade, and other measures promoting individual liberty, was the political agency of the middle-class will. And the Second Reform Bill (1867), followed by Gladstone's great ministry of 1868–74, marked the triumph of middle-class rule. Their defeated enemies could only lament, as Matthew Arnold did, that with general acceptance of the bourgeois "notion of its being the great right and happiness of an Englishman to do as far as possible what he likes, we are in danger of drifting towards anarchy. We have not the notion, so familiar on the Continent and to antiquity, of *the State,*—the nation in its collective and corporate character, entrusted with stringent powers for the general advantage, and controlling individual wills in the name of an interest wider than that of individuals."[36]

So it seemed in 1868—but the actual consequences of the ascent of the bourgeoisie to power proved ironic. In the wake of the two Reform Bills, they found that they *were* "the State," and the assertion of its "stringent powers" through the rule of law no longer seemed antithetical to the assertion of their individual wills. Thus, in 1869, "large elements in the middle classes," metamorphosed into proponents of government control, were alienated by Gladstone's proposal for disestablishment of the Irish Church, and thereafter cast their lot with the Conservatives. Free trade became a dying issue, as "tariff barriers and other discriminatory measures . . . were erected with increasing frequency and height" during the century's last two decades.[37] Once Gladstone's ministry ended in 1874, middle-class support kept the Conservatives in power through eighteen of the twenty-seven remaining years of Victoria's reign: only a general shift in bourgeois allegiance could have offset the massive increase in Liberal voters resulting from the Third Reform Bill's enfranchisement of millions of laborers in 1884.

In short, however radical had been their attacks on the established order while they were still arriving, the late Victorian bourgeoisie became its conservative defenders once they had arrived. And their most ardent desire was now to blend with their betters:

> *The new middle class, unlike the old, was sensitive about its status, and perpetually sought to pass for something other than it was. The Philistines of Matthew Arnold had been proudly and aggressively class-conscious; like Mr. Pickwick, they were not ashamed of being middle class. But the new bourgeoisie, unforgettably pictured in the Veneerings of Dickens'* Our Mutual Friend, *were "brand-new people in a brand-new house in a brand-new quarter of London," and were rather uneasy about it. They educated their sons to be as nearly as possible like what they thought the sons of the aristocracy were.*

Thus, the ruling passion of the middle class became the lust for respectability. "Indeed," remarks Walter E. Houghton, "their economic struggle was focused less on the comforts and luxuries which had hitherto lain beyond their reach than on the respect that money could now command." But the purchase of this commodity could not be effected without renunciation of that "great right . . . to do as far as possible" just as one pleased. "Here," as Richard Altick observes, "individualism ceased. Respectability was not subject to private definition; its attributes represented a consensus. They included sobriety, thrift, cleanliness of person and tidiness of home, good manners, respect for the law, honesty in business affairs, and, it need hardly be added, chastity."[38] Actuated by a desire to prove to the world that their new status had been achieved as much by means of moral desert as sharp business practice, the middle class became more demonstratively, rigidly, and self-denyingly obedient to written and unwritten social and civic codes of behavior—which I shall collectively refer to as "law"—than any other segment of English society. The corollaries of this obedience were obvious: respect for law's magistrates in society and respect for its parental surrogates in the microcosm of the family. The consequences for the arts included widespread bourgeois hostility against works that failed to embody this peculiar moral perspective.

Still, the perspective in question was not entirely new but

merely more coherent: the righteousness of duty and the wickedness of self-gratification had also been important tenets of the Evangelicalism that had coexisted so oddly and uneasily with Utilitarianism in the minds of the earlier nineteenth-century bourgeoisie.[39] Nor were the pressures of this perspective unfelt by the earlier nineteenth-century theater. Thus, it is not surprising to find that George Colman the Younger, who served from 1824 to 1836 as the government censor to whom all dramatic manuscripts were submitted before production, officially objected "to any play the plot of which concerned rebellion."[40] What is surprising is that this philosophical prejudice allowed him ever to license a single comedy.

For over 2,000 years—since the appearance of Greek New Comedy, its subsequent propagation by the Romans, and its eventual domestication by Shakespeare and his successors—the dramaturgical tradition passed down to the Victorian comic theater had unequivocally favored rebellion. The norms of comedy's plots had come to include: the triumph of the self-will of the young over any restrictive codes of behavior or laws that opposed their erotic choices; the defeat, and sometimes humiliation, of those magisterial and parental figures who attempted to enforce these codes; and, ultimately, the wholesale displacement of the social order with which both these authority figures and their codes were identified. Thus, Frye's formulation of the Victorian ethical ideal, with its exaltation of obedience of the ego to authority, stands in sharp contradistinction to his description of the prejudices of comedy, in which "At the beginning of the play the obstructing characters are in charge of the play's society, and the audience recognizes that they are usurpers. At the end of the play the device in the plot that brings hero and heroine together causes a new society to crystallize around the hero."[41] Nor was the vitality of this insurrectionary tradition on the wane as it entered the nineteenth century. Susanne K. Langer sees it nakedly embodied in a figure popular on the street corners and at the fairs of the time, "the English Punch, who carries out every impulse by force and speed of action—chastises his wife, throws his child out of the window, beats the policeman" and thus appeals "to people's repressed desires for general vengeance, revolt, and destruction."[42] But Punch was not content to live outdoors only; as will presently be seen, his spirit, the spirit of traditional comedy, lurked also in every important form of nineteenth-century comic drama. Hidden amidst elaborate scenery and costumes, highly developed acting styles, and occasionally even witty dialogue, it may have been less immediately recognizable than it was in the puppet plays, but it was no less antagonistic to Victorian middle-class values.

"The action of comedy," says Frye, "moves from law to liberty"; its plot pattern consists in a "movement from . . . a society controlled by habit, ritual bondage, arbitrary law and the older characters to a society controlled by youth and pragmatic freedom." And the claims of law, as Maurice Charney states, are reduced by such plots to the status of problems: "The institution of law—much favored as a comic subject—does not enunciate immutable truths. . . . In comedy, human considerations always triumph over law, so that any insistence on the letter of the law, like Shylock's harping on his bond, is doomed to failure. The comic spirit is meant to prevail over mere technicalities, but the technicalities are usually invoked at the beginning of a comedy to provide the obstacles that must eventually be overcome."[43] Such tales are what the audiences of comedy have traditionally been asked to endorse with their applause. It is little wonder that the Victorian bourgeoisie, whose ethical center was respect for law, sat on their hands or, more frequently, on their drawing-room sofas, at home and safe from the moral contagion of the comic theater.

If the standard plotting of comedy must have aroused middle-class hostility, the standard characterization must only have increased it. For comedy delights in placing its protagonist at the head of the devil's party:

> *If we separate respectable, upstanding citizens from the anarchic, irresponsible, and hostile world of comedy, we find not just two opposing views of reality, but rather two warring camps. . . . This is an appropriate place to raise the nagging question of whether comedy is cruel. It is certainly antisocial, if by society we mean to indicate the prevailing values. Comedy is almost always by its*

very nature destructive and anarchic, and the comic hero tries to make his hesitant way outside the norms of society. He may have a new, mad vision that society must listen to in order to survive, but he is still an outcast and pariah. Comedy is cruel because it takes a position apart from morality and accepted standards. The comic hero feels threatened by these criteria, and he doesn't agree to play by the rules. In an effort to survive, he engages in relentless, guerrilla warfare with society.

And, of course, he wins. At the same time, his opponents—those characters who attempt to uphold the established order—are exposed as *alazons,* or impostors, for the moral basis of their claim to authority is rejected by such comedy as spurious. Prime among them is "the *senex iratus* or heavy father, who with his rages and threats, his obsessions and his gullibility, seems closely related to some of the demonic characters of romance";[44] such, in traditional comedy, is the less than honorific depiction of law's surrogate within the family. His efforts are, of course, directed toward keeping the hero and heroine apart, and he is often assisted by society's magistrates, as Theseus supports Egeus in *A Midsummer Night's Dream.* These agents of the law take on the father's guilt by association; others, such as Angelo in *Measure for Measure,* emerge as impostors in their own right. As this latter example suggests, the characters in comedy whose power places them in authority or judgment over others are often revealed to be not just "usurpers" but hypocrites. Adherence to morality proves no more typical of them than of the hero.

Thus, Victorian middle-class sentimentality—with its preference for art marked by "the exaggeration of the benevolent character through bestowing on it an incredibly warm heart that irradiates the soul with extraordinary kindness and pity"—can have found few gratifying objects among traditional comedy's characters. But virtue is not the standard by which these characters are normally meant to be judged; their appeal, rather, consists in their energy. "The buffoon," for instance, is "the indomitable living creature fending for itself, tumbling and stumbling (as the clown physically illustrates) from one situation into another, getting into scrape after scrape and getting out again, with or without a thrashing. He is the personified *élan vital.* . . . He is neither a good man nor bad one, but is genuinely amoral." Similarly, his first cousin, the fool, "a red-blooded fellow . . . close to the animal world" with a symbolic "cockscomb on his cap . . . is all motion, whim, and impulse—the 'libido' itself."[45]

Here we begin to glimpse yet another aspect of that energetic activity which figures so importantly in traditional comedy's rebelliousness and yet another reason that such comedy can only have made respectable Victorians squirm. For Frye asserts that "The action of comedy is intensely Freudian in shape; the erotic pleasure principle explodes underneath the social anxieties sitting on top of it and blows them sky-high. . . . In comedy we see a victory of the pleasure principle that Freud warns us not to look for in real life." But the sexual impulse, as embodied in the hero, is not merely given the victory in comedy; it is also invested with moral authority. Why is the audience expected to be pleased when the hero gains possession of the heroine? Our pleasure has little to do with the appeal of his personality; indeed, the tendency of comedy is "to play him down and make him rather neutral and unformed in character." Rather, the true source of our sympathy is most clearly revealed when we see this hero compete, as he often must, against "a rival with less youth and more money" whose "claim to possess the girl must be shown up as somehow fraudulent."[46] To label one man's desire "fraudulent" and another's valid may of course seem absurd, as if lust has moral gradations. But we must remember here the context of the hero's ultimate triumph: the final scene which not only "brings hero and heroine together" but also "causes a new society to crystallize around the hero" and, in so doing, holds forth the promise of a better future for that society as a whole. This promise may be fulfilled only one way, and now we know why we feel "right" about the hero being at the girl's side: his youth and vitality make him a fitting biological partner for her, and we prefer that he, rather than the apparently less virile old man, should father her children.

Moreover, we actually feel that we have a stake in the matter. Langer proposes that comedy "expresses the continuous balance of sheer vitality that belongs to society and is exemplified briefly in each individual"; if the hero and heroine stand for all of us, we want to feel the greatest possible confidence in their reproductive future, for they represent our larger hope for the perpetuation of the species itself. The assurances we seek are normally forthcoming, for it has traditionally been comedy's business to affirm life's continuity:

> *The same impulse that drove people, even in prehistoric times, to enact fertility rites and celebrate all phases of their biological existence sustains their eternal interest in comedy. . . . The sense of precariousness that is the typical tension of light comedy was undoubtedly developed in the eternal struggle with chance that every farmer knows only too well—with weather, blights, beasts, birds, and beetles. . . . The essential comic feeling . . . is the sentient aspect of organic unity, growth, and self-preservation.*

While the preservation of the hero's self, and that of his society, may crown the stage action of comedy, "the essential comic feeling" extends beyond the footlights. For, as the audience enters into "communion" with the cast at the end of a comedy and we indicate by our applause that we have accepted the play's implicit "invitation . . . to form part of the comic society,"[47] the self whose preservation we cheer expands to include the whole of our own society and, through "organic unity," the whole of the human race.

In most ages, a request that the audience affirm its faith in the perpetuity of the species would have seemed innocent and joyful enough. But in the Victorian age, it could easily have inspired anxiety—especially among the more educated social classes, who were well aware of the extent to which science had been clouding this very issue with doubt:

> *According to the second law of thermodynamics, announced in 1850 and immediately adopted by Dickens for the running imagery of* Bleak House, *the irreversible conversion of energy to heat in the cosmos will ultimately turn it into a lifeless mass of incandescence. According to some geologists, similarly, the earth, having passed through the creative phase in which mountains and seas were formed, now had entered the final stage of process, "decrepitude" or*

disintegration. In the face of this postulation of universal and irreparable decay, the Victorians' confidence in the ongoing, divinely ordained improvement of man's estate could not but seem shallow, narrow, and petty—not to say ill founded. Combined with the parallel tendencies of evolutionary theory, these intimations of cosmic mortality contributed to the somber hue of some late Victorian poetry and of fiction like Hardy's.

But this was merely the culmination of a darkening that had begun even before Victoria's ascension. Faith that man is forever had been overclouded at least since Charles Lyell had published his *Principles of Geology* (1830–33), the second volume of which grimly insisted that "the reader has only to reflect on what we have said of the habitations and the stations of organic beings in general, and to consider them in relation to those effects . . . resulting from the igneous and aqueous causes now in action, and he will immediately perceive that, amidst the vicissitudes of the earth's surface, species cannot be immortal, but must perish one after the other, like the individuals which compose them." And the effects of such ideas were soon apparent in literature. In a famous passage of *In Memoriam,* published in the same year that the second law of thermodynamics was revealed, Tennyson imagined Nature concurring with Lyell:

> "So careful of the type?" but no.
>   From scarped cliff and quarried stone
>   She cries, "A thousand types are gone:
> I care for nothing, all shall go."[48]

Nine years later, when Darwin published his *Origin of Species*—with its notions of "natural selection" and "survival of the fittest" implying that man, as now formed, might eventually be superseded, displaced, and exterminated[49]—Victorians were given additional scientific cause to wonder whether their species, like others before it, was marching toward extinction. Going to a theater and clapping for a comedy which asked one to affirm one's faith that the matter stood otherwise became correspondingly more difficult.

Darwin's work, of course, cut deep into the soul of his age: it challenged not only the Victorians' faith in the permanence of their species but also their more fundamental faith in the existence of their God. This, too, had implications for the credibility of comedy. To be sure, comedy had always strained the limits of credibility; as Frye admits, "Happy endings do not impress us as true, but as desirable, and they are brought about by manipulation." But the suspension of disbelief necessary to audiences' acceptance of such endings had always been made possible by appeal to an overarching belief:

> In comedy where there is a sense of violent manipulation of plot, of characters leaping into new roles, or events driving towards a renewing transformation in the teeth of all probability, it is easy to arrive at moral axioms about a divine providence. Thus in Gascoigne's Supposes . . . one of the characters turns out to be, according to a frequent New Comedy device, the son of another character, stolen from him in infancy. This provokes the reflection from the father: "And you, Philogano, may think that God in heaven above ordained your coming hither at this present, to the end I might recover my lost son whom by no other means I could ever have found out." The remark inspires an equally sententious rejoinder: "Surely, sir, I think no less, for I think that not so much as a leaf falleth from the tree without the ordinance of God."[50]

In short, the comedic tradition that Victorian dramatists inherited was distinctly theistic. Though God may not always receive as much explicit credit from nineteenth-century characters as he does from Gascoigne's, the superintendence of Providence is unmistakably implied by all endings which involve coincidence, last-minute reversals in fortune, sudden repentances, and the like. The standard plot of comedy may move from law to liberty, but divine law ensures human freedom, as in the Christian Bible's scheme of redemption. In comedies postdating the Middle Ages, we rarely find endings that hinge upon particular points of religious dogma, but they normally assume a consensus among the audience about the fundamental fact of Providence.

The late Victorian period was the first in western culture in which such a consensus had begun to crumble. Faith in the truth of revelation had been eroded by the same scientific questioning that had broken down faith in the future of the species: "If only the Geologists would let me alone," wrote Ruskin in an 1851 letter, "I could do very well, but those dreadful Hammers! I hear the clink of them at the end of every cadence of the Bible verses." The volume of this dismal music was intensified during the next decades, as the scientific evidence against Scripture continued to mount. *Origin of Species* was followed in 1868 by T. H. Huxley's "Physical Basis of Life," which "carried *The Fortnightly* into a seventh edition" and "left the religious mind prostrate and quivering with horror"; Darwin's own *Descent of Man* (1871) met with only dispirited opposition. The informed and educated classes knew they had a choice to make between "the supreme Victorian value of truth-telling"— the virtue which would lead a reasonable human being to acknowledge the force of scientific argument—and "the faith in which one had been reared, and to which one's family had subscribed without question for many generations."[51] Such a choice was necessarily agonizing, and all who confronted it must have felt periodically tempted, if not quite to yield up moral questions in despair, at least to seek a respite from them. With cinema and television still in the distant future, what better escape was available to a bourgeois Victorian of the seventies than to take in a light comedy at one of London's newly refined and accessible theaters?

Here, however, he would encounter an interesting irony. Settled in his recently reupholstered stall, gazing down on a tastefully decorated set, this hypothetical theatergoer might have felt comfortable enough to laugh at much of the two hours' traffic of the stage—until the final minutes, when he would have found himself confronted by the very choice that he had come to the theater to avoid. For now the rituals of the playhouse called upon him to validate the happy ending; as Frye notes, the fall of the curtain requires an "act of communion" between actors and audience, such that "The resolution of comedy comes, so to speak, from the audience's side of the stage."[52] As long as traditional comedy and its Providential denouements continued to hold the stage, the invitation to communion essentially demanded that the audience either affirm (by applauding) or deny (by sitting on its hands) its faith in divinity itself. Such issues were debated and actually put to formal votes at the Metaphysical Society meetings of the seventies, but no Victorian who came to the theater seeking intellectual escape can have relished being called by Harlequin to a division on the same question. Of course, few theatergoers would have been fully conscious of casting a ballot on God's existence, but any who now found themselves regarding comic drama as somehow unconvincing or unsatisfactory may have felt vaguely uneasy about why they responded thus. It is not unlikely that they sensed the clink of the geologists' hammers and the creak of the *Beagle*'s timbers echoing in each constrained clap of their hands.

Clearly, this was not a situation likely to create an enthusiastic following for comedy. Nor, as we have seen, would any important aspect of traditional comedy have seemed congenial to the nineteenth-century English bourgeoisie: with its anti-legal plots, its energetically rebellious heroes, its debased authority figures, its unblinking optimism about the perpetuity of the species, and its solidly theistic assumptions, traditional comedy simply did not embody a moral and intellectual consensus to which the respectable, educated middle classes could subscribe. And, as Henri Bergson has remarked, participation in such a consensus is essential to the enjoyment of comedy:

> *Our laughter is always the laughter of a group. . . . A man who was once asked why he did not weep at a sermon when everybody else was shedding tears replied: "I don't belong to the parish!" What that man thought of tears would be still more true of laughter. However spontaneous it seems, laughter always implies a kind of secret freemasonry, or even complicity, with other laughers, real or imaginary. How often has it been said that the fuller the theatre, the more uncontrolled the laughter of the audience! On the other hand, how often has the remark been made that many comic effects are incapable of translation from one language to another, because they refer to the customs and ideas of a particular social group!*[53]

Given their values, the Victorian middle class must have felt much like foreigners in the English theater. No "freemasonry" could exist between them and the denizens of pit and gallery, who, as a legitimately oppressed proletariat, would hardly have been offended by rebellious themes or characters; and who, as a predominantly un-educated group, would scarcely have been troubled by the theoreti-cal findings of scientists or their intellectual disagreements with religious scholars. Unable to join in the communion of laughter, the bourgeoisie abandoned the parish. While traditional comedy remained ascendant in the theater, the Victorian middle class oc-cupied its leisure hours at home.

There, of course, they amused themselves with novels, many of which were also comedies. But the values espoused by these works were, arguably, different fundamentally from those en-dorsed by Victorian stage plays. For, as D. A. Miller suggests, the presiding genius of the nineteenth-century novel was the "disci-plinary power" subsequently described by Michel Foucault:

> *It is the policing power that never passes as such, but is either invisible or visible only under cover of other, nobler or simply blander intentionalities (to educate, to cure, to produce, to de-fend). . . . In more general terms, the discretion of social discipline in the Novel seems to rely on a strategy of* disavowing the police: *acknowledging its affinity with police practices by way of insisting on the fantasy of its otherness. Rendered discreet by disavowal, dis-cipline is also thereby rendered more effective—including among its effects that "freedom" or "lawlessness" for which critics of the Novel (perpetuating the ruse) have often mistaken it. Inobtru-sively supplying the place of the police in places where the police cannot be, the mechanisms of discipline seem to entail a relative relaxation of policing power. No doubt this manner of passing off the regulation of everyday life is the best manner of passing it on.[54]*

Thus, in the work of the middle class's, and Gilbert's, favorite novelist, Miller notes that Rose and Mrs. Maylie refuse to co-operate with the police when they come to ask questions about Oliver Twist, and yet they prepare the boy for "full integration into middle-class respectability" by exerting total control over his schedule and education: "the techniques that structure Oliver's time are precisely those of a domesticating pedagogy."[55] Thus, too, we may interpret the interplay of external compulsions upon Pip's efforts to save Magwitch: while his task is entirely unsanctioned by the law of the police, it nonetheless appears to him in the form of a duty, and he unwillingly takes it up as such. The result, of course, is that the hero learns humility, and it is only when his offensive egotism is squelched (as a traditional comic hero's would never be) that he is morally prepared to assume his proper place in society as both worker and husband.

Indeed, Herbert argues that Dickens increasingly dissociated himself from the spirit of traditional comedy, especially by refusing to accept its "paramount feature . . . the orientation toward pleasure":

> In later novels Dickens's pleasure-lovers like "Gentleman" Tur-
> veydrop, Harold Skimpole, or Henry Gowan emerge as among
> his most despicable characters . . . while all moral approval is
> channeled to such figures of self-denying stoicism as Agnes Wick-
> field, Esther Summerson, and Amy Dorrit. The deepening pu-
> ritanical cast of Dickens's writing is unquestionably the medium of
> his greatest works of imagination, but all the magnificence and
> moral exuberance of novels like Bleak House and Little Dorrit
> come surrounded with a melancholy moral ethos that condemns
> pleasure and lightness of heart. . . . In setting out his radical vision
> of the social and spiritual crisis of modern Britain, Dickens, like all
> other prophets, sacrifices certain dimensions of his own human-
> ity—and, for all his inspired use of farce, grotesque humor, and
> satire, estranges himself altogether from the unifying vision of
> comedy.[56]

Of course, Dickens's practice and perspective were not those of every Victorian novelist; at the same time, none of his competitors commanded the loyalty—and shillings—of the bourgeoisie as he did.

On the other hand, the tendencies of the major genres of Victorian stage comedy would have provoked this portion of the public to quite the opposite of loyalty. The anti-legal prejudices of such comedy were perhaps most blatant in the pantomimes of the early decades of the century; as Michael R. Booth suggests, these displayed "a general hostility toward constituted and inherited authority" which was "manifested . . . in vicious treatment of an oppressive father figure, Pantaloon, and his watchman or police-man surrogate" and offered their audiences "a release for sadis-tic impulses toward cheating, tricking, larceny, cruelty, wanton destruction, violence, and rebellion." And though the form was somewhat sanitized as the century progressed—"probably for the edification of the increasing number of children in the audience," such that "a fixed moral pattern became apparent in the opening"— criminality remained the behavioral norm in the harlequinade. Moreover, the standard conflict of pantomime remained what Hil-ary Thompson calls "The battle between youth and the established order of the day . . . epitomized by the need of lovers to over-come the disapproval of parents and of older characters"[57]—the same need that drove the action of such "pure" comedies as Bouci-cault's *London Assurance* (1841), Robertson's *Society* (1865) and *Caste* (1867), and James Albery's *Two Roses* (1870).

Nor was "extravaganza" a true departure from traditional comedy. To be sure, when J. R. Planché evolved this new genre from pantomime, he consciously aimed at reform and refinement: his major structural innovation was the exclusion of the harle-quinade, pantomime's most explicit celebration of anarchy. But an anti-legal thrust remained implicit in his plays, undermining their aspirations toward respectability. Frequently, the action of his pieces revolves around some curse or other legalistic edict that must be, and is, overturned: such is the case in *The Sleeping Beauty in the Wood* (1840), *Beauty and the Beast* (1841), and *The Island of Jewels* (1849). Frequently, too, in adapting well-known stories, Planché would alter the endings to spare his characters from the punish-ments of laws both human and divine: such is the case in *Olympic Revels; or, Prometheus and Pandora* (1831), *Blue Beard* (1839), and *The Golden Fleece; or Jason in Colchis and Medea in Corinth* (1845). His delicacy, wit, and classical learning raised him above his competi-tors in extravaganza and burlesque, but he was unable consistently to attract the patronage of lucrative audiences: after more than fifty years of "prodigiously industrious" activity in the theater and over 150 plays, "a Civil List pension of £100 a year" was nonetheless "a matter of importance to him."[58]

While Planché may have hoped to win the favor of polite society, the social ambitions of Victorian farce were considerably less lofty. Rather, it was written primarily for and about the proletariat who remained faithful to the playhouses throughout the century, and its anti-legalism, consequently, was far from subtle. Typical of its characters is the tailor Widgetts, who is motivated through the whole of John Stirling Coyne's *How to Settle Accounts With Your Laundress* (1847) by a desire to escape from law, seeking first to evade his legally binding promise to marry Mary White and later to avoid capture and conviction for a crime he did not commit. Also typical are the waiter Veskit in William Brough's and Andrew Halliday's *The Mudborough Election* (1865), who ultimately achieves happiness by accepting a political bribe, and the printer Box and hatter Cox, title characters of John Maddison Morton's famous 1847 piece, who are only persuaded to stop quarreling by a mutual unwillingness to submit their dispute to the arbitration of a court. Like Widgetts, all three of these men seek to flee the contractual bond of betrothal; unlike the outwitted tailor, they fortuitously succeed. Writers of farce felt no ambiguity about the malignity of law: happiness consisted in dodging its judgments and shunning its restrictions and obligations.

The antagonism of the melodramatists was even more overt. As G. Wilson Knight remarks, the early nineteenth-century variety of this genre grew "from a soil of accepted valuations opposing low-born simplicity and virtue to a villainous squirearchy, tyrannic landlords, and legal cruelty" and embodied "an implicit criticism of a system dominated by financial power supported by law."[59] Thus, we find William, the sailor-hero of Jerrold's *Black Ey'd Susan* (1829), dipping into his bottomless well of nautical metaphor to rant against "His Beelzebub's ship, the Law!"; thus, we also find Claude Melnotte, a peasant and philosophical Radical, triumphant over both an aristocratic rival and bourgeois snobbery in Bulwer-Lytton's *The Lady of Lyons* (1838). And though later decades saw the proletarian sympathies of melodrama tempered by the desire to please the newly accessible middle class, the heroes of Boucicault's three greatest Irish dramas—*The Colleen Bawn* (1860), *Arrah-na-Pogue* (1864), and *The Shaughraun* (1874)—were all either outlaws

or rebels against the English. Moreover, the plots of such plays—
like those of farce, and like those of nearly every important "pure"
comedy of Robertson's—continued through the century to be
founded on the sort of Providential coincidence that educated,
post-Darwinian audiences can no longer have readily accepted.

Even the early works of Gilbert and Sullivan substantially
subscribed to the principles of traditional comedy. The supreme
authority figures of *Thespis* (1871) are cast in a far from honorific
light: according to the stage directions, the celestial Diana first
appears "wrapped up in . . . Shawls" with "a respirator in her
mouth, and galoshes on her feet" (9); the radiant Apollo is "an
elderly 'buck' with an air of assumed juvenility" (9); and the once
mighty Jupiter has been reduced to "an extremely old man, very
decrepit" (11).[60] Indeed, so ungodlike have these gods become that
they are technically *alazons,* for their symptoms of decay and weak-
ness suggest that their claim to immortality and power is an imposture. Their replacement on Olympus by Thespis's company of
actors, or professional impostors, seems appropriate.

Moreover, the players' change of identity in the Act I finale
clearly derives from pantomime, that most virulently anti-legal
form of Victorian comedy, which likewise featured a transformation scene about midway through each piece. And the spirit of the
harlequinade evidently informs the year that passes before the start
of Act II, as we learn that these "gods" have run riot since their
metamorphosis, ignoring the customs and restrictions that ought
to govern their divine behavior. However, the finale to the second
act brings a second transformation, as Thespis and his troupe are
condemned by Jupiter to become "eminent tragedians / Whom no
one ever, ever goes to see!" (25) and, with this curse, are exiled from
the fantastic and free world of Olympus back to the mundane, law-
bound earth. As in most traditional comedies, the edicts of authority and the rule of law are associated with unhappiness.

Accordingly, disregard of the law ensures the happiness of the
protagonists in *Trial By Jury* (1875). The Judge freely confesses that
he owes his professional success to improper, if not unlawful,
dealings: "It was managed by a job" he sings of his rise to the
judiciary, "and a good job too!" (37) His present conduct reflects nc

greater honor on either his position of authority or the law he represents, as he hypocritically ascends the bench to sit in judgment on a breach of promise, a crime which he cheerfully boasts of once having gotten away with himself. And he displays a clear contempt for his own court in refusing to take time to bring the current case to a proper conclusion: "I can't stop up here all day," he declares, "tossing his books and papers about" (40). Thus, he literally throws away the law. In determining to abort the trial by marrying the Plaintiff, he acts upon the traditional comic hero's preference for fulfilling lust instead of law, and yet his conduct goes entirely unpunished, as the story closes with his embrace of his bride. Indeed, as if to underline the dramaturgical tendencies of this piece, Gilbert borrowed a leaf from pantomime for an 1884 revival, adding a "Grand Transformation Scene" in which the Judge became Harlequin, the Plaintiff Columbine, and the curtain descended amidst a blaze of red fire.[61]

The Sorcerer (1877), however, shows Gilbert continuing to use, but beginning to question, the patterns of traditional comedy. The title character, John Wellington Wells, is employed by Alexis, the hero, to administer a love potion which causes each unmarried male in Ploverleigh to fall in love "with the first lady he meets who has also tasted it, and his affection is at once returned" (61). But when its magic impels the heroine not into Alexis's arms but rather those of the village rector, the hero wants the spell revoked. Wells explains that this can be achieved by "one means" only: "Or you or I, must yield up his life to Ahrimanes" (68). Unfairly, the assembled citizenry designates Wells, the instrument, rather than Alexis, the instigator, as the victim. "The potion's law" (68) is thus overturned, and the young hero is enabled to marry the young heroine, but this standard comedic resolution is purchased at a terrible price: the unjust sacrifice of another life. Like Gilbert's earlier *Broken Hearts* (1875) and the later *Yeomen of the Guard* (1888), *The Sorcerer* may be a traditional comedy, but it is not an entirely happy play. Imbued as the author himself was with the Victorian bourgeois ethos, he may well have been starting to wonder whether these two categories were mutually exclusive.

And he must certainly have been wondering whether any

material advantage might be derived from continuing to write such pieces. *Trial By Jury* and *The Sorcerer* each had a respectable initial run of 175 performances, but this did not represent a vast improvement over *La Vivandière* and *The Merry Zingara,* two burlesques with which Gilbert had, a decade earlier, achieved runs of 120 performances each. Except for *Pygmalion and Galatea* (1871), few others of his plays had enjoyed significantly more success. Clearly, traditional comedy—whether written with or without Sullivan— could be made to yield little more than mediocre receipts from a nineteenth-century box office.

Still, there was one dramatist whose success on the Victorian stage occasionally transcended mediocrity, perhaps because polite society made his plays an exception to its general rule of theatrical abstinence. This was Shakespeare, whose popularity among such audiences may at first seem odd, for it is arguable that no other author's work is so clearly marked by the dramaturgical tendencies that I have associated with traditional comedy; indeed, much of the comic theory articulated by Frye and others is grounded upon Shakespearean practice. So, too, did many Victorian playwrights inevitably refer to Shakespeare, the English prototype of post-Aristophanic New Comedy, as a model for their own work; as a result of following his anti-legal lead, they found themselves excluded from bourgeois favor. Yet Shakespeare's own appeal was undeniable: as Alan S. Downer observes, "the rising spirit of 'Bardolatry'" made him nothing less than "the leading playwright of the nineteenth century."[62]

Nevertheless, certain productions of his work attracted polite audiences more readily than others: "The Opera was respectable," affirms George Rowell, "and Shakespeare, when performed by Macready or Charles Kean, might become so."[63] No two managers were more closely connected with the movement toward antiquarianism—the use of sets and costumes scrupulously faithful to the historical period of each play's story—and here, I believe, we find the key to their audiences' anomalous acceptance of Shakespeare's dramaturgy. In addition to gratifying their taste for spectacle, the stage illusion of living history permitted them a psychological distance from the action, and this became crucial when that action was comic. If laws and magistrates were successfully defied, they were only authorities of centuries past. If young lovers in Renaissance dress were joined together in a union with implicit promise for the future of the species, the audience had no reason to question the validity of the promise: after all, the race had survived 300 years since their mating. And if God's miraculous help was involved in bringing the lovers together and rewarding their friends, one might merely sigh with a pleasant cultural nostalgia for the faith of one's ancestors, which had held such things to be possible.

To endorse the happiness of a safely remote Hermia or Florizel was one thing; to cheer the triumphs of rebellious young lovers in modern dress was quite another. And, by mid-century, the dominant trend in the production of original plays was toward emphasizing their contemporaneity by attempting to duplicate on stage the mundane details of Victorian life. Ingratiating as this practice might have been—especially in Robertson's "cup-and-saucer" pieces of the sixties—it also had its drawbacks. "The nineteenth century dislike of realism," wrote Wilde in 1891, "is the rage of Caliban seeing his own face in a glass," and the statement held particularly true when the mirror was comedy and the reflection colored by comedic tradition. On the whole, audiences preferred to gaze directly upon Caliban himself.

Rump Steak and Oyster Sauce

How, then, did Gilbert distinguish himself from his predecessors and competitors and eventually come to rival even Shakespeare in the chaste affections of the Victorian middle class? Various answers have been proposed; each embodies an element of relevant truth, but none provides a fully sufficient explanation of his success.

Some have said that Gilbert and Sullivan led the reform movement that brought the playhouses back within the pale of polite society and made the act of theatergoing respectable again.[64] This is less than a half-truth. The battle had, in fact, been fought and won in the half-century preceding *Pinafore;* Gilbert and Sullivan were merely fortunate enough to appear in time to collect the spoils. The first important blows were struck by Madame Vestris, the renowned actress and singer who took over the management of the

Olympic Theatre in 1831 and made it, according to Planché, "a life-boat to the respectability of the stage, which was fast sinking in the general wreck." Her productions were widely praised for their taste and meticulous attention to detail, which lent them a charm and refinement lacking at the more licentious houses that aimed mainly at the achievement of broad, "vulgar" effects. In addition, Vestris nurtured the careers of others who were to make significant contributions to the reform movement. Her leading actor—eventually her husband and partner—was Charles James Mathews, who is generally credited with introducing a more delicate and "gentlemanly" style of playing to the nineteenth-century comic stage. Her favorite author was Planché who "was lucky enough to find in Madame Vestris a manager who shared his aim of refining both the style and the staging of classical burlesque," and whose extravaganzas "did much to raise the tone of 'illegitimate' comedy and, incidentally, to prepare the way for W. S. Gilbert."[65] And her prompter at the Lyceum, the last theater she managed, was Tom Robertson, whose gently humorous plays of middle-class life lured the bolder bourgeoisie of the sixties to the Prince of Wales's Theatre; it was also Robertson, according to Gilbert, who originated the practice of imposing artistic unity on a production through painstaking stage direction. In short, Vestris and her tribe left little work for Gilbert, Sullivan, and D'Oyly Carte to do toward the purification of either the decorum or decor of the English theater. But the efforts of these reformers failed to attract the kind of patronage that made their Savoy successors rich: neither Planché nor Robertson ever became wealthy, while Vestris and Mathews were perennially bankrupt. Clearly, respectability was not enough.

Some have said that Gilbert's work was simply better than that of other Victorian dramatists, but such an assertion reveals more about the tastes of the asserter than it does about the plays in question. It does not explain to me why certain plays that my own tastes rank among Gilbert's best—*Tom Cobb* and *Engaged,* for instance—proved relatively unpopular, while such a tired libretto as that of *The Gondoliers* led to one of his biggest hits. Moreover, while the best works of Robertson, Boucicault, and Planché may not have been equal to Gilbert's masterpieces, they do not seem to me inferior in the same proportion that their authors' profits were. Quality, I think, was not enough.

Some have said that Gilbert owed much of his fame and fortune to his collaboration with Arthur Sullivan, unquestionably the greatest English composer of his era. But Sullivan, too, was not enough. His scores for other talented playwrights failed to add a Midas touch to their librettos: neither F. C. Burnand's *The Contra-bandista* (1867), nor Sydney Grundy's *Haddon Hall* (1892), nor *The Beauty Stone* (1898)—despite contributions to the last by so distin-guished a dramatist as Pinero—achieved very long runs. Nor, indeed, did the first three pieces for which he supplied music to Gilbert: even for him, Sullivan did not represent a surety of success.

But this is not to denigrate the composer. Rather, a quantita-tive assessment of each partner's contribution to the collaboration suggests that primary responsibility for the success or failure of any given piece ought to be assigned to the librettist. Unlike grand opera, in which the music is omnipresent, at least one-third of each Savoy opera (except *Trial By Jury*) is dialogue: Gilbert without Sullivan. Moreover, it was Gilbert who devised and directed the whole of each piece's stage action and who superintended the design of costumes and sets. As Sullivan himself once ruefully remarked, "They are Gilbert's pieces with music added by me."[66]

The procedure that Gilbert and Sullivan used in constructing their works confirms the composer's statement. Again, a useful contrast may be drawn to the practices prevalent in nineteenth-century grand opera, for which the libretto was written expressly to serve a musical conception. Among Sullivan's older and younger contemporaries on the continent, one finds Verdi ordering verses from Piave in much the same spirit as a gentleman might give a shoemaker his specifications for boots; one also finds Puccini re-sorting to no fewer than five librettists for *Manon Lescaut* and finally finishing the book himself in order to get precisely what he wanted. In general, the average operatic composer had no doubt that the opera was his particular property and that the librettist was not a partner but rather an employee who did his work under direction. Conversely:

The Gilbert and Sullivan method of collaboration appears to have followed the following pattern: First the author described to the composer his idea for a plot, or he read him a plot outline. Then, if Sullivan responded with enthusiasm, Gilbert wrote out a complete story-line, without dialogue and without lyrics. . . . Next, working painstakingly through trial and error on scores of copybook pages, he roughed out his libretto, including the lyrics, which he sent to Sullivan for setting as fast as they were finished. . . . In Gilbert's own words, when interviewed by William Archer: "The verse always preceded the music, or even any hint of it."

One feels little wonder that Sullivan complained of having his role reduced to mere "syllabic setting" or that he longed after doing "a work where the music is to be the first consideration—where words are to suggest music, not govern it."[67]

Of course, Sullivan's music transcended "syllabic setting," and the contribution made by its brilliance to the popularity of the Savoy operas should not be undervalued. But neither should his estimation of his own relative importance to the collaboration be dismissed. If his music exerted enormous appeal, it did so within the context of a structure that had been conceived and built by Gilbert.

I maintain that it is in the unique architecture of that structure that we may find the answer to the question about the source of Gilbert's unparalleled popularity. And the crucial point about this architecture is that it was planned with the sole view of achieving such popularity, and the money that came with it. One cannot fully understand the nature of Gilbert's mature comic dramaturgy without first recognizing the mercenary aim that prompted its development.

Naturally, loyal fans of the Savoy operas have resisted this notion, preferring to believe that their favorite plays were shaped according to some Platonic form of the Comic, but most critics have recognized Gilbert's true motivation. Isaac Goldberg notes that "In later years we find him sharply interested in the box-office receipts of the pieces at the Savoy. When he came to the United

States he was careful to tell reporters how well this play had done, how much money that one had made for him." Jane Stedman concurs, contending that "Gilbert had a very healthy respect for profits, whatever else he made fun of." And Hesketh Pearson puts the case quite bluntly: "All his writing was done for money, and he never pretended another reason for it."[68]

Nor did Gilbert himself mince words on this matter. Toward the end of his career, he told an acquaintance, "I have been scribbling twaddle for thirty-five years to suit the public taste." And he refused to accept compliments that suggested otherwise. When Alfred Austin wrote to him upon the occasion of the widely lauded premiere of *The Gondoliers,* Gilbert replied with "Many thanks for your kind congratulations. The piece is ridiculous rubbish and is, accordingly, hailed as a masterpiece. If it had deserved one-half of the encomiums passed upon it, it would have been howled off the stage." Similar sentiments informed "a conversation of Gilbert's later days with a visitor who was admiring the beauty of his home, Grim's Dyke. 'Are you not very proud of having acquired all this out of your own brain?' asked the visitor. 'Not at all,' said Sir William, 'it represents the folly of the British public.'"[69]

Contemptuous though he professed to be, Gilbert clearly recognized that his success was founded upon giving this public what it wanted. Nor was this success the product of luck or accident; rather, he claimed to have conceived his works with the preferences of his patrons at the forefront of his mind. Indeed, in an 1894 interview, he claimed actually to have attempted, for their sake, to keep down the literary quality of his plays:

> *A knowledge of stage-craft, and faculty of laying on one's colours with breadth and discretion are, in my opinion, the keynotes of success. If I were capable of writing intellectual dialogue of a high order, I should use that power very rarely, and I should administer such dialogue in homeopathic doses, for it would be absolutely wasted on nineteen-twentieths of the audience. The press would be particularly severe upon me—they always resent anything that is (to them) incomprehensible. My usual course is to assume that I am writing for the edification of a sensible but somewhat stolid*

individual, to whom everything must be made perfectly clear and distinct. Such a man is a fair type of an average English audience.

Likewise, in 1885 when an interviewer asked him, "In writing comic opera and other things what do you think of first?" Gilbert stated his guiding principle succinctly: "Generally, I think . . . what is in demand, or I think is in demand."[70]

In focusing on the demands of "the average English audience," Gilbert placed his primary emphasis on satisfying the bourgeoisie, the embodiments of the Victorian social mean. And, in the spirit of modern marketing, his approach to developing a product that would appeal to this targeted group was fully systematic:

> *A man who sets to work to cater for the entertainment of theatrical audiences is in the position of a refreshment contractor who has engaged to supply a meal of one dish at which all classes of the community are to sit down. What should that dish be? It must not be* suprême de caille *or it will be regarded as insipid by the butcher-boy in the gallery. It must not be baked sheep's head or it will disgust the epicure in the stalls. It must, I suppose, be some dish that will fit the gastronomic mean of the audience, and I take it that that gastronomic mean will be somewhere in the neighborhood of rump-steak and oyster sauce. If I am right in this conjecture, it seems to follow that a dramatist who intends that his profession shall furnish him with an ample income should confine himself to writing plays of the rump-steak and oyster sauce description.*

James Ellis comments thus on this manifesto: "As shrewd a businessman as Carte himself, Gilbert felt his audience's pulse with professional skill. . . . Whatever compromise with artistic principles may have been involved, Gilbert almost invariably geared his comic operas to that dictator of popular taste, the middle-class businessman."[71]

How, then, did he gain this dictator's favor? I will argue that Gilbert could never have attracted and kept the allegiance of the middle class without first subverting the spirit and content of the comedy which Shakespeare and his nineteenth-century heirs had established as "traditional" on the English stage. And I will attempt to extract the fundamental principles of the comedy that Gilbert custom-made for the Victorian bourgeoisie, and to explain how the resultant "modified rapture" manifested itself in his most successful works: the series of librettos for Sullivan that began with *H.M.S. Pinafore*—the "high Savoy operas"—and that mark the fullest development of his mature comedic method.

II

---·◦∞◦·---

The High Savoy Operas

*Law, Laughter, God and Nature: Basic Principles of
Gilbert's Comic Dramaturgy*

PERHAPS GILBERT'S RESPONSE to traditional comedy is most clearly
revealed by his comments on two of its most important representatives on the Victorian stage: Shakespeare, to whom nineteenth-
century dramatists looked as a model, and pantomime.

About Shakespeare, Gilbert's pronouncements verged on the
virulent. In a 1904 letter, he professed himself as "bored by *The
Tempest* as I was by *Richard II* and *Julius Caesar,* three ridiculously
bad plays. I daresay Shakespeare was a great poet. I am not qualified
to express a technical opinion on that point, but I consider myself an
authority on dramatic work and I have no hesitation in expressing a
professional opinion that all his works should be kept off the
boards." As this sweeping condemnation suggests, Gilbert found as
little to admire in Shakespeare's comedies as in any of his other
works. Indeed, the comedies seem to have been particularly on his
mind when he once confided to George Grossmith: "If you promise
me faithfully not to mention it to a single person, not even to your
dearest friend—I don't think Shakespeare rollicking."[1]

But it is likely that the true source of Gilbert's negativity was
that he did not think Shakespeare profitable. However successful
the antiquarian productions of the century's earlier decades may
have been, by 1879—as *Pinafore* was in the midst of its lucrative run
at the Opera Comique—the financially beaten F. B. Chatterton was
abandoning the Drury Lane with the cry that "Shakespeare spells
ruin" to a theatrical manager.[2] And, more important to Gilbert, the
unprosperous fates of those nineteenth-century dramatists whose
own plays followed Shakespeare's anti-legal lead furnished ample
evidence that little money was to be made from contemporary
recensions of traditional comedy.

Nor is it surprising that, of all these recensions, pantomime should have attracted Gilbert's special antipathy, for in no other form was the antisocial soul of comedy laid quite so bare. Even before his own playwriting career was well underway, Gilbert's attitude emerged in a number of his Bab ballads. There we find the title character of "The Story of Gentle Archibald" influenced by the example of a Clown he has seen on stage to embark on a joyless career of mayhem and murder; there, too, we find the speaker of "Pantomimic Presentiments" expressing his thorough boredom with the form's conventions, and the speaker of "At a Pantomime" plunged by the performance into thoughts of poverty, sickness, and death. But perhaps Gilbert's most pointed indictment of the genre is contained in an 1864 essay for *Fun* entitled "On Pantomimic Unities." Foremost among his complaints were the violence with which pantomime is rife and the impunity with which its perpetrators defy civic law. "Is clown mortal or immortal?" asked Gilbert. "He appears to possess the privilege of doing whatever he likes to the constituted authorities without fear of any unpleasant consequences. This is the way in which he usually treats policemen prior to knocking their heads off, which is murder; but nobody ever heard of a clown being hung or even condemned to death." And he was not at all pleased with this rascal's treatment of Pantaloon, the debased persona which the paternal authority figure of the opening would normally assume after the transformation scene: "He suffers fearful indignities at the hands of clown. . . . He is buffeted, insulted, and bullied in an insupportable manner." In another 1864 piece, entitled "The Physiognomist at the Play," Gilbert identified the true target of Clown's violence: "When a tinker appears on the stage we all know that the clown is going to burn Society with that tinker's hot iron."[3]

Even in the later decades of the century, when pantomime labored to achieve respectability, Gilbert refused to accept its new pretensions. In his 1881 farce *Foggerty's Fairy,* the protagonist is about to drink a magic potion given him by Rebecca, the title character, but he hesitates:

> FOGGERTY: There's one question I should like to ask—This is not a pantomime?

REBECCA: Bless the man, no.

FOGGERTY: It won't end in my being changed into Harlequin, and Jenny into Columbine, or any nonsense of that sort, will it? Because if it does—

REBECCA: You need not alarm yourself. This is not a Pantomime, but a very graceful and poetical Fairy Extravaganza. Rather dull, perhaps, but quite refined, and containing nothing whatever that could shock the sensibilities of the most fastidious.[4]

For Gilbert, pantomime and "refined" comedy ever remained mutually exclusive categories.

But, at the same time that he was inveighing against the genre, he was also writing in it. His early work for the stage included a pantomime of his own, *Harlequin Cock-Robin* (1867), and contributions to two others. It also included melodrama, providentially resolved "pure" comedy, farces adapted from naughty French originals, a proto–problem play attacking middle-class hypocrisy (*Charity* [1874], which was "denounced as immoral for its sympathies with the 'fallen woman' "), and numerous burlesques. Clearly, in the first fifteen years of his playwriting career, Gilbert either had not yet determined to ingratiate himself with the bourgeoisie or had not yet discovered the dramaturgical means of doing so. And yet, as Granville-Barker speculated about the last of the operatic burlesques, *The Pretty Druidess* (1869), "Gilbert must have known from the beginning—how should he not?—what this burlesque game was worth, and now he is pretty certain that the game is up. And the history of his career, in its consequence to the English theatre, is the history of his creating something of permanent value (though intensely individual and not to be further developed after him) out of the wreck and rubbish of it; Savoy opera, that is to say."

To be sure, the plays of the next nine years—and even *The Pretty Druidess* itself—show Gilbert experimenting with many of the ingredients of his mature comedic formula. But it was not until the experiment embodied in *Pinafore* met with unsettling success that Gilbert was moved to abandon altogether the traditional comedic models and devote himself to developing a new one. Writing for western civilization's first post-theistic era, Gilbert approached his

task in the post-theistic spirit later defined by Friedrich Dürrenmatt: "Comedy—in so far as it is not just satire of a particular
society as in Molière—supposes an unformed world, a world being
made and turned upside down, a world about to fold like ours. . . .
the comical consists in forming what is formless, in creating order
out of chaos."[5] Gilbert brooded over this abyss and determined to
make human law the ordering principle of his comedic universe,
inserting it into the role that tradition had reserved for the gods or
God in the comic dramaturgy of his predecessors.

I use the term "human law" in a broad sense, for I mean it to
include not just the written rules enacted by governments but rather
all formal and informal codes of behavior that become sources of
external compulsion to the characters of the operas and that are
distinguishable from individual will on the one hand and divine
decrees on the other. Thus, the carefully spelled-out articles of
apprenticeship that bind Frederic to the Pirates of Penzance, the
marriage contract that bound Casilda to her infant bridegroom
many years before the action of *The Gondoliers* begins, and the
unwritten aesthetic *dicta* that oblige Grosvenor to act as a trustee for
Beauty and Patience to love none but an imperfect man are all
included under this definition. So are the witch's curse that governs
the world of *Ruddigore* and the fairy law that hovers over the action
of *Iolanthe:* they may be supernatural in their operations or origin,
but they ultimately become human instruments when they prove
susceptible to reinterpretation and amendment by mortals. The
particular forms assumed by these many compacts and codes are
varied and fanciful, but they are a constant presence in the operas.

Specifically, Gilbert places a markedly untraditional valuation
upon human law in three crucial areas of his mature comic dramaturgy. If such law occasionally represents a problem for his characters, it almost unfailingly provides them with a solution; thus, the
first of Gilbert's comedic reforms was to replace the traditional law-
to-liberty pattern with plots in which the sympathetic characters
achieve happiness as a direct result not of defying but rather of
satisfying and submitting to the law. Again, if traditional comic
heroes are aggressive rebels against law while its enforcers are
hypocrites and impostors, Gilbert's heroes either are or become

passive slaves to external compulsion. At the same time, his magisterial and parental authority figures are almost all benign. His characters, in short, either fall in line with law or derive credit from their identification with it. Finally, if traditional comedy normally culminates in the crystallization of a new society around a young couple whose union promises the perpetuation of life, Gilbert makes the fulfillment of some superintending law, rather than of love, the ultimate objective of his comic action. The next three sections of this chapter will discuss each of these three dramaturgical practices.

The centrality of law to Gilbert's comedy may well have been a reflection of the status it occupied in his life. In the years before his literary career truly began, he had embraced the law as a personal and professional savior:

> *I obtained, by competitive examination, an assistant clerkship in the Education Department of the Privy Council Office, in which ill-organized and ill-governed office I spent four uncomfortable years. Coming unexpectedly into possession of a capital sum of £300, I resolved to emancipate myself from the detestable thraldom of this baleful office; and on the happiest day of my life I sent in my resignation. With £100 I paid my call to the Bar (I had previously entered myself as a student at the Inner Temple), with another £100 I obtained access to a conveyancer's chambers; and with a third £100 I furnished a set of chambers of my own, and began life afresh as a barrister-at-law.*

In his mature comedy, law was similarly to provide a haven for characters fleeing from various forms of "detestable thraldom." And, despite his failure to flourish as an attorney, he never ceased to trust in law as an arbiter: as a modern Lord Chancellor has observed, Gilbert was himself "one of the most prolific litigants of his time. Unlike most lawyers, when Gilbert was aggrieved he turned to law as a first, instead of a last resort."[6] The apologia that he offered for it in the Savoy operas was, thus, as congenial to his own sensibilities as to those of the bourgeoisie he sought to please.

Still, one aspect of Gilbert's practice has led many critics to reject the notion that his librettos contain any such apologia. Max

Keith Sutton, for example, holds that the operas are devoted to "ridicule of legalistic attitudes" and that "Gilbert illustrates Northrop Frye's assertion that 'the action of comedy . . . is not unlike that action of a lawsuit,' and that it often develops in response to 'some absurd, cruel, or irrational law.' "[7] Indeed, we find it impossible to deny the absurdity of many of the laws that govern the Savoy operas—even though they do, after all, dictate the happy endings. Thus, Ellis argues that Gilbert's humor is based upon "the tendency for rules to take precedence over human needs" and that he presents "the contention of an inelastic system with ever-varying life," intending that his audiences should be "amused by the inadequacy of the response of the former to the latter."[8] And so we are. At the same time, the characters themselves remain blissfully unaware of any such inadequacy; thus, our vicarious participation in their happiness becomes curiously mixed with laughter at their amiably impaired understanding of the applications and implications of the laws that solve their problems. Even where the law itself is not intrinsically absurd, the obedience of such servants tends to render it ludicrous.

The most striking example occurs in *Utopia (Limited),* where the climactic scene finds the South Sea Islanders complaining that the adoption of English law and custom has so perfected their country that the military, legal, and medical professions—all of which depend upon human imperfection—have been rendered unnecessary. In typical high-Savoy fashion, Princess Zara, who has been the moving force behind the Anglicizing of the island, responds to the protest of her countrymen not by overturning the sociolegal system but rather by amending it. All that is required, she explains, is the addition of a single item which she had previously forgotten:

> *Government by Party! Introduce that great and glorious element—*
> *at once the bulwark and foundation of England's greatness—and*
> *all will be well! No political measures will endure, because one*
> *Party will assuredly undo all that the other Party has done; . . . and*
> *while grouse is to be shot, and foxes worried to death, the legisla-*
> *tive action of the country will be at a standstill. Then there will*

(412)

be sickness in plenty, endless lawsuits, crowded jails, interminable confusion in the Army and Navy, and, in short, general and unexampled prosperity!

The enthusiasm with which the princess's auditors cheer her latest legal dispensation causes us to laugh at their joy, even as we share in the happiness that her reforms make possible for the sympathetic characters. Similarly, when Grosvenor is compelled by Bunthorne to transform himself from a perfectly beautiful being into a commonplace and generally unattractive young man, Patience responds to his alteration with wholehearted joy, as she can now return his love without violating the rule she has learned about loving unselfishly. We are delighted to see a man and a woman who have pined for one another finally united, but we are simultaneously aware of the absurdity of a code that holds one ineligible to be loved unless one is unlovable.

Broadly speaking, the means by which Gilbert elicits laughter at law take two distinct forms, each of which is essentially a species of dramatic irony. We are made to laugh when we perceive, while the characters remain oblivious to, logical flaws in their applications of the law; and we are made to laugh when we see these characters unthinkingly and mechanically cleave to the letter of the law in cheerful unconcern that, by so doing, they are completely subverting its original intention and spirit. Neither method was original to Gilbert, and each may be illuminated by reference to a classic work of literary theory: the former receives attention in Aristotle's *Poetics,* while the latter is central to Henri Bergson's discussion of *Laughter,* written a few years after the end of Gilbert's collaboration with Sullivan.

In *Poetics* 16, Aristotle lists the six forms of "discovery" that a dramatic poet might use to resolve a plot, and it is the fifth of these—discovery by "false inference" or faulty reasoning—that is especially relevant to Gilbert's practice in his Savoy curtain scenes. Aristotle maintained that these false inferences, though understood by the poet to be untrue, may be entirely innocent on the part of the characters who make them: "A mistaken recognition might occur," explains Lane Cooper, "when no deceit was intended."[9] That such errors in reasoning abound in Gilbert's denouements has long been recognized. For instance, Kim A. Emmence has pointed out inconsistencies in the legal logic of *Iolanthe:* for one, if Strephon is half a fairy, then in the first act (when the law against fairies marrying mortals is still in force) the Fairy Queen ought not to bless his intention of marrying the thoroughly human Phyllis; for another, when the Peers, Lord Chancellor, and Private Willis are all transformed into fairies at the end of the opera, they are immediately disqualified as mates for the female fairies, who are now operating under the law that any fairy must die who does *not* marry a mortal.[10] But the characters themselves notice none of this and, sincerely believing that law has sanctioned their marriages, fly happily off to Fairyland. Similarly, Ko-Ko resolves the plot of *The Mikado* when he proves to the monarch that, despite spilling no blood, he has actually satisfied the royal demand for an execution: "It's like this: When your Majesty says, 'Let a thing be done,' it's as good as done—practically, it *is* done—because your Majesty's will is law. Your Majesty says, 'Kill a gentleman,' and a gentleman is told off to be killed. Consequently, that gentleman is as good as dead—practically, he *is* dead—and if he is dead, why not say so?" Though the thoroughly mollified monarch replies that "Nothing could possibly be more satisfactory!" (268) as all launch into the joyful finale, more stringent logical analysis might have suggested to him that accepting Ko-Ko's argument also entails accepting that his son, the announced victim of the execution, is legally dead, and this in turn means that Ko-Ko and his comrades should still be boiled for compassing the death of the Heir Apparent. Again, though, the characters remain happily ignorant that they have logically failed to fulfill the law. But the more alert audience laughs, just as it does at *H.M.S. Pinafore*'s climactic revelation that Captain Corcoran and Ralph were switched in their cradles when both were infants, which the principals blithely accept without any puzzlement over how the former has since managed to father a daughter little younger than the latter, who has somehow managed to remain a "youth" (82).

Frequently, in order to call attention to their logical missteps, Gilbert has his characters express their legalistic reasoning in nearly formal terms: as Sir Roderic remarks in *Ruddigore,* "these arguments sound very well, but I can't help thinking that, if they were reduced to syllogistic form, they wouldn't hold water" (297). Indeed, all the elements of a syllogism are present in Ko-Ko's decisive argument, which may be formalized thus:

> MAJOR PREMISE: A thing which is the Mikado's will is a thing which is as good as done.
> MINOR PREMISE: An execution is a thing which is the Mikado's will.
> CONCLUSION: Therefore, an execution is a thing which has been done.

The living presence of Nanki-Poo during this explanation immediately helps the audience to detect the flaw: "a thing which is as good as done" does not mean quite the same thing as "a thing which has been done." In formal logical terms, Ko-Ko's conclusion introduces a fourth substantive term into this syllogism, which, like all categorical syllogisms, can validly contain only three.[11]

Turning to Gilbert's hypothetical syllogisms, we find it useful to refer again to Aristotle, who, in the *Poetics,* discusses the problem of how a poet should artistically present a lie:

> *The essence of the method is the use of a logical fallacy. Suppose that, whenever A exists or comes to pass, B must exist or occur; men think if the consequent B exists, the antecedent A must also— but the inference is illegitimate. For the poet accordingly, the right method is this: if the antecedent A is untrue, and if there is something else, B, which would exist or occur if A were true, one must elaborate on the B; for, recognizing the truth of the added details, we accept by fallacious inference the truth of A.*[12]

In *Patience,* Lady Angela unknowingly becomes the mouthpiece for just such a lie, as she explains why she and the other rapturous maidens have followed Archibald Grosvenor's lead in abandoning aestheticism in favor of commonplace dress and behavior: "Archibald the All Right cannot be all wrong; and if the All Right chooses to discard aestheticism, it proves that aestheticism ought to be discarded" (165). Angela's error is to assume that free choice has preceded Grosvenor's transformation—which, as the audience knows, was actually forced upon him by Bunthorne—and her mistaken inference of the antecedent thus leads her to what must be regarded as a false conclusion. Meanwhile, Gilbert amply elaborates on the consequent, stipulating a complete change of costume and demeanor for Grosvenor and the entire women's chorus; modern productions frequently take up Gilbert's hint and give the formerly cultured poet a Cockney accent. At the same time, as in the other Savoy operas, logical fallacy does not here prove to be incompatible with happiness: indeed, though the ladies may erroneously arrive at their acceptance of the behavioral code of mainstream society, this change in attitude propels them into the arms of the dragoons.

Still, while the formal rules of logic may help us to pinpoint the places in which Gilbert's characters err in their deductive applications of general principles and laws to specific problems and circumstances, an academic knowledge of these rules is hardly necessary to detect the presence of such errors. Audiences with no notion of what a syllogism is can sense the illogic of Ko-Ko's contention that a thing not done is essentially the same as a thing done. Likewise, it is clear enough that his mode of obeying the Mikado's legal demand for an execution entirely subverts the spirit of that decree and frustrates its original intention.

But even Gilbert's formally valid deductive constructs may leave us with the uneasy feeling that something is logically amiss. In *Iolanthe,* the fairies have been operating under a law that every fairy must die who marries a mortal, but once the Lord Chancellor persuades the Fairy Queen to amend this to "every fairy shall die who *don't* marry a mortal" (201), valid deductive logic not only sanctions but requires each of the marriages that the fairies have already concluded with the peers. And, in *Ruddigore,* when Robin finally propounds his argument that, under the terms of the witch's curse, "A Baronet of Ruddygore can only die through refusing to commit his daily crime" so that "to refuse to commit a daily crime is tantamount to suicide" which "is, itself, a crime" (303), it follows quite logically that all of Robin's ancestors who died as a result of the curse ought actually to be alive, and the opening-night version of the opera accordingly featured the resurrection of the first twenty-one baronets, along with general mating and rejoicing.

But, happy as these endings are, and formally valid though the syllogisms authorizing them may be, we cannot quite shake the awareness that each of these legalistic solutions begins with an indefensible major premise. The Lord Chancellor entirely perverts the spirit and substance of fairy law when he transmutes "every fairy must die who marries a mortal" into its contrary, while the statement about the "only" way a baronet of Ruddigore can die requires us to believe that the members of the Murgatroyd family are exempt from all ordinary laws of mortality. The characters themselves, however, are untroubled by any misgivings; rather, they accept and apply the laws with unthinkingly rigid obedience.

This mechanical mode of following even ridiculous rules is the second of the major means by which the legalism of Gilbert's characters invites our laughter. The nature of such humor has been probed by the theories of Henri Bergson, a writer who, like Gilbert, was fundamentally concerned with the transactions between the spirit of comedy and the spirit of the nineteenth-century bourgeoisie. As Wylie Sypher observes:

> One cannot read Bergson's essay [on laughter] without remembering what Marx said in 1848: that the middle class has deprived man of his individuality and made him an appendage to the machine. Bergson . . . saw this very danger and remarked that "regulating life as a matter of business routine is more widespread than might be imagined." . . . Bergson spent all his philosophy protesting against the mechanical, seeking to discern in us "the individuality that escapes our ken," attempting to protect what is inward and spontaneous from what is automatic. To Bergson laughter is an exposure of our ready-made gestures and values, and the comic figure is one who is not a man but, instead, a clockwork apparatus leading the special kind of life a puppet seems to have.

In Bergson's own formulation, the "laughable element" consists in "a certain *mechanical inelasticity* just where one would expect to find the wideawake adaptability and the living pliableness of a human being." This inelasticity can be physical, as exemplified in a person who stumbles and falls because he has failed to adapt his movements to obstacles in his path, or mental, as exemplified by a Don

Quixote who follows a fixed idea. And Bergson considers the
audience's laughter at the mishaps that befall such characters to be
a way of punishing their unthinkingly mechanical behavior: "In
laughter we always find an unavowed intention to humiliate, and
consequently to correct our neighbour."[13]

Bergson's notion of laughable behavior is clearly embodied in
those Savoy characters whose rigid and unreflective obedience to
law surely qualifies as intellectual inelasticity. Perhaps the most
striking instance occurs in the finale of *H.M.S. Pinafore*. Its climax
comes when Buttercup reveals that Ralph and Captain Corcoran
were exchanged in the cradle, and it therefore follows that the sailor
has a legal right to whatever aspects of his commander's identity
derive from birth alone. "Wideawake adaptability" might sort
matters out on this basis and determine that, while Ralph is entitled
to recognition as a member of a higher social class and to the family
wealth which mistakenly became Corcoran's, nothing else ought to
change. But "wideawake adaptability" is nowhere to be found
among the *dramatis personae* of *Pinafore,* and the newly discovered
legal fact is mechanically and indiscriminately applied to *all* aspects
of the two men's characters: as Stedman observes, "externals, tem-
peraments, non-ancestral rank, [and] acquired characteristics are
made contingent upon known, not actual identity, and if everyone's knowledge of the identity changes, these characteristics also
change."[14] The Major-General takes the same tack at the end of *The
Pirates of Penzance:* when he learns that the title characters are,
legally, peers and persuades them to shed their identities as outlaws,
all their moral defects seem to vanish from his sight and he enthusiastically embraces them as sons-in-law.

But the crucial fact remains that the denouements resulting
from these mechanical applications of legal facts, like those enabled
by logically flawed deductions from the law, are happy ones. This
was merely to be expected from a dramatist whose aim was not to
attack but rather to justify the bourgeois ethic, including the middle-class tendency toward "regulating life as a matter of business
routine." In other words, unless we inexplicably suppose Gilbert's
humor to have been working at cross-purposes with his plots—
which *reward* even ridiculous reliance upon law—it is unlikely that

the laughter he elicits by Bergsonian means was intended to serve the Bergsonian end of correcting such regulated behavior and humiliating its exponents.

Indeed, an illuminating parallel may be found in the practices of Gilbert's prosody, in that his lyrics for the Savoy librettos are just as rigidly regular in fulfilling the requirements of rhyme scheme and meter as his characters are in obeying the law. Sometimes, explicit attention is drawn to this: three times during the Major-General's patter song in *The Pirates of Penzance,* the stage directions indicate that he stops because he is "bothered for next rhyme" and cannot or will not proceed until "struck with an idea" of what that rhyme should be (120–22); similarly, in *The Grand Duke,* when the Notary rhymes "lowest" with "ghoest," he pauses to explain that "When exigence of rhyme compels, / Orthography forgoes her spells, / And 'ghost' is written 'ghoest' " (429). But while this torturing of language into prosodic regularity was clearly intended to invite laughter, it evoked ridicule neither for the lyricist nor for the characters he made his mouthpieces; rather, it was and is regarded as one of the chief sources of Gilbert's peculiar poetic felicity—just as complete obedience to law is productive of happiness in the plots of his operas. Thus, when Jones Hewson, the Herald in the premiere of *The Grand Duke,* sang a solo in which the sole distinctive feature of the lyrics was the frequency with which they were contorted for the sake of meter and rhyme (accenting the final syllables of "also" and "Monte Carlo," and changing the pronunciation of both "particular" and "auricular" to create a rhyme with "stickler" [467]), his number "unexpectedly caught both press and audience" and was "dubbed by the *Times* 'one of the most taking things in the opera.' " Likewise, in *Iolanthe,* Private Willis emphasizes his obedience to the demands of the rhyme scheme by use of four pairs of highly conspicuous triple rhymes in his one song; though his entire role includes little more than this song, Audrey Williamson observes that "There can be no doubt in the mind of anyone who has sat in a contemporary theatre, that Private Willis still takes second place only to the Lord Chancellor in the affections of the audience."[15] Far from provoking derisive laughter, the Procrustean prosody of his song, and the humor thus created, help to earn him a popularity far out of proportion to his importance in the piece.

Nor did the original audiences of the operas feel called upon to detach themselves from the festivity of Gilbert's curtain scenes and to sneer at the unthinking mechanical rigidity that had made them possible. Rather, as A. F. Marshall remarked in an essay published some months after the premiere of *The Mikado,* "His art is to show you how you *might* laugh at folly, if you flung the rein over the neck of your irony; while, at the same time, he seldom moves out of his gentle amble, seldom uses a spur or a whip. Hence there is no fatigue, no reaction. *He* enjoys quiet; so do *we.*"[16] Most modern critics have concurred with this assessment. Eighteen years after Gilbert's death, Ashley Thorndike stated what has remained the prevailing view:

> *Gilbert was a middle-class Victorian tory of many crotchets and prejudices. He endured without great dissatisfaction most of the things that he laughed at. He had humour enough to see something funny in many things, but he also had humour enough to know that almost anything is funny when looked at upside down. He did not hold things upside down as an argument that they were useless. His banter and irony were intended to reach the average intelligence but not to alarm or disrupt it.*[17]

In short, though Gilbert may have invited his audiences to laugh at the law, he did not do so in the punitive spirit of corrective satire.

What other end might this laughter then serve? Bergson suggests that the significance of laughter consists in its impact upon its object, but others have emphasized the importance of laughter for the laugher. Cooper, for instance, supposes that Aristotle "would think that comedy in providing us with its specific pleasure, and by arousing laughter, gave occasional vent to certain passing emotional states, and thus left us free for the serious concerns of life. By comedy then, we should be cured of a desire to laugh at the wrong time, and at the wrong things, through being made to laugh at the proper time by the right means."[18] In other words, Aristotle would probably have argued that comedy, like tragedy, leads to a catharsis for the audience, achieved through laughter. In our own time, psychoanalytic theory has embodied a similar idea. As Sypher notes, Freud's *Wit and Its Relation to the Unconscious* holds that "the joke, like the dream, is an upsurge from the unconscious, a mechanism for releasing powerful archaic impulses always there below the level of reason." And such release is essential to the social conformity of both the joker and his audience: "We have a compulsion to be moral and decent, but we also resent the obligations we have accepted. The irreverence of the carnival disburdens us of our resentment and purges our ambivalence so that we can return to our duties as honest men."[19]

But there are, I think, other psychic forces that the catharsis of laughter may help us to expend and therefore control. For there are longings and misgivings which are primarily rational in origin and must, like our animalistic desires, be repressed if we are to get on with the day-to-day business of our lives; no less than our more inchoate impulses, they irritate the underside of our consciousness and would probably fester there if not given an occasional opportunity to break through. Their specific shape has varied from age to age, depending mostly upon what new uncomfortable facts science has recently forced human reason to confront. But if twentieth-century men and women need the laughter of *Dr. Strangelove* in order to learn how to stop worrying about teleology and love the bomb, so the educated classes of the late Victorian era needed help in coming to terms with science's destruction of their cherished faith in a God who had given order and meaning to their lives. And Gilbert's comic method constituted a response to just this need: he offered his audiences imperfect human law as a replacement for a perfect Providence, yet simultaneously encouraged them to laugh at this substitute and thus purge their reservations about its adequacy.

To be sure, unlike such late Victorian sages as Arnold and Pater, who were fairly explicit in proposing that the void left by God's disappearance be filled by culture or art, Gilbert never actually acknowledged that any such substitute was necessary. Yet Christian Providence is conspicuously absent from the world of the high Savoy operas and from the consciousness of the characters who dwell therein. Rather, we find Josephine polytheistically invoking both the god of love and the god of reason in *H.M.S. Pinafore*, Grosvenor appealing to Chronos in *Patience*, and Princess Ida praying to Minerva for help in educating her students. Even when he created an entirely serious dramatic situation, in which stage prayer could not have been construed as blasphemy, and set it in the Protestant context of Tudor England, Gilbert refused to allow Elsie to call upon the God of Christianity, having her rather apostrophize Mercy as she waits for Fairfax to be led to the block in *The Yeomen of the Guard*. Nor are the earlier operas any more orthodox: it is the demonic Ahrimanes whose unseen presence dominates *The Sorcerer*, while the gods and goddesses of *Thespis* are borrowed (and burlesqued) from Roman mythology.

The deities of *Thespis* have become so outmoded and remote from mankind that they must be replaced by mortal agents; their status, in other words, is not much different from that which was accorded the Christian God in the post-Darwinian Victorian mind. In Gilbert's more mature librettos, the displacement of the divine by the human is more tactfully managed; still, though it is only implicit, it is essential to the structure of his dramaturgy and decisively distinguishes him from his predecessors. In the tradition that Gilbert inherited, "Unlikely conversions, miraculous transformations, and providential assistance" had been "inseparable from comedy."[20] Such was certainly the case in Shakespeare, whose work defined for nineteenth-century audiences the norms of comedy; such was also the case in every genre, from melodrama to farce, in which Victorian dramatists produced original plays. But in Gilbert's high Savoy operas, the peripety—the reversal in fortunes that renders the sympathetic characters happy—is always presented as the effect of a distinctly human cause. In *Patience, Iolanthe, Princess Ida, The Mikado, Ruddigore, Utopia (Limited)*, and *The Grand Duke*, the satisfactory resolution depends upon the reinterpretation or amendment or fresh explanation of some existing law, and in each case the saving insight is supplied by human ingenuity (or, at least, research). In *H.M.S. Pinafore, The Pirates of Penzance*, and *The Gondoliers*, a last-minute revelation of legal identity contributes decisively to the general happiness of the characters, but no melodramatic last-minute coincidence sparks the revelation: neither

Buttercup nor Ruth nor Inez is suddenly brought in by Providence or enlightened thereby in the final scene; rather, each is available as a source of information from an early point in her play, and each is persuaded to give up her secret by the turn that events have taken. In short, Gilbert sends in human ingenuity, or simply human knowledge, as the cavalry to rescue the deserving. And law is this human savior's chief weapon, just as Providence is God's in traditional comedy.

Within the boundaries of his comedic world, Gilbert's savior was no less efficacious or morally sound than traditional comedy's had been. For the man-made rules and codes invoked in the Savoy finales resolve each plot and subplot just as neatly, and mete out justice and mercy just as fairly, as Hymen does in *As You Like It* or Jupiter does in *Cymbeline*. Here, however, Gilbert was venturing upon philosophically shaky ground. The impact of the evolutionists had been profound, and the last decades of the nineteenth century were consequently marked, as Houghton observes, by "the scientific view that all things, material and human, were in constant flux, changing under the inevitable influences of many and complex factors"—a view which tended to "make all truths seem relative only to a particular moment."[21] The late Victorians, in short, found it difficult to subscribe to faith in the absolute reliability of *any* arbiter, and their new skepticism was no less pertinent to the "truths" propounded by society and its laws than to those declared by the church and its scriptures.

But here we return to the crucial function of laughter at law. Gilbert could hardly have expected his skeptical patrons to readily accept any flawed, man-made code as a fully adequate substitute for the divine dispensation which they had held to be perfect as long as they could believe it to be real—and yet, the confession of human law now represented the only available alternative to moral anarchy. But the catharsis of laughter facilitated acceptance of the new order: when Gilbert's characters unthinkingly or mechanically applied human law to problems it could not actually solve, the law's limitations were highlighted and the audience permitted to laugh away their discomfort about just these limitations. Purged of misgivings about the mortal imperfections of such law, these audiences would have left the theater more cheerfully inclined to obey it. Gilbert's irony thus becomes not merely decorative but crucial to his comic method. And Gilbert's denouements would further have reconciled his bourgeois patrons to their highly regulated way of life by suggesting that their obedience was worth the self-sacrifice and temporary frustrations it might entail, for it inevitably led to happiness. This delicate manipulation of attitude and feeling was unique to Gilbert, and it accounts, I think, for his unique success in the nineteenth-century theater.

Indeed, nobody has more cogently explained the nature of the result aimed at by the Gilbertian approach to comic catharsis than Gilbert himself, in a scene in *Utopia (Limited)*. Law here is embodied in King Paramount who, though actually under the thumbs of his two wise men, is perceived by the Utopian populace as "A King of autocratic power . . . / A despot whose tyrannic will is law" (388). These wise men have forced Paramount to write and produce a comic opera entitled "King Tuppence; or, A Good Deal Less than Half a Sovereign" in which, as Phantis reminds the reluctant author, "the celebrated English tenor, Mr. Wilkinson, burlesques your personal appearance and gives grotesque imitations of your Royal peculiarities" (391). But when the King expresses his distress over such a "horribly personal" performance, Scaphio explains that this ludicrous portrayal of the monarch actually strengthens the authority of the law he represents: "Why consider: During the day, thousands tremble at your frown; during the night (from 8 to 11), thousands roar at it. During the day your most arbitrary pronouncements are received by your subjects with abject submission—during the night, they shout with joy at your most terrible decrees. It's not every monarch who enjoys the privilege of undoing by night all the despotic absurdities he's committed during the day" (391). Gilbert's own comic operas aimed to confer upon the written and unwritten laws and codes governing Victorian behavior the same privilege that the wise men force Paramount to earn for himself.

But Gilbert's purposes in promoting human law went beyond proposing it as a substitute for Providence, for his librettos also assigned to it the place of honor which traditional comedy, with its

exaltation of impulse and instinct, had reserved for Nature. While
the earlier nineteenth-century "romantic sensibility had found the
divine spirit rolling through all things, and had worshipped nature
as the nurse and guide of life," the scientific evidence that subsequently challenged the Victorians' faith in the Creator likewise
undermined their trust in his creation. In the wake of Lyell and
Darwin, "nature became a battleground in which individuals and
species fought for their lives and every acre of land was the scene of
untold violence and suffering"; thus, now it was perceived as
"indifferent to all moral values, impelling all things to a life of
instinctive cruelty ending in death."[22] By 1874, even John Stuart
Mill, whose opinions on the subject could not be dismissed as mere
by-products of a lapsed faith in God ("I am," he declared, "one of
the very few examples in this country of one who has not thrown
off religious belief, but never had it"), was found, in a posthu-
mously published essay, arguing thus:

> *The word Nature has two principal meanings: it either denotes the*
> *entire system of things, with the aggregate of all their properties, or*
> *it denotes things as they would be, apart from human intervention.*
> *In the first of these senses, the doctrine that man ought to follow*
> *nature is unmeaning; since man has no power to do anything else*
> *than follow nature; all his actions are done through, and in*
> *obedience to, some one or many of nature's physical or mental laws.*
> *In the other sense of the term, the doctrine that man ought to follow*
> *nature, or in other words, ought to make the spontaneous course of*
> *things the model of his voluntary actions, is equally irrational and*
> *immoral. Irrational, because all human action whatever, consists*
> *in altering, and all useful action in improving, the spontaneous*
> *course of nature: Immoral, because the course of natural phe-*
> *nomena being replete with everything which when committed by*
> *human beings is most worthy of abhorrence, anyone who endeav-*
> *oured in his actions to imitate the natural course of things would be*
> *universally seen and acknowledged to be the wickedest of men.*[23]

It is in the context of this intellectual climate that we need to read
such works as *Trial By Jury,* produced the year after Mill's essay was

published, in which Gilbert has the Defendant offer this plea to excuse his jilting the Plaintiff for another lady:

> Oh, gentlemen, listen, I pray, I pray,
>   Though I own that my heart has been ranging,
> Of Nature the laws I obey,
>   For nature is constantly changing.
> The moon in her phases is found,
>   The time and the wind and the weather,
> The months in succession come round,
>   And you don't find two Mondays together.
>   Consider the moral, I pray,
>   Nor bring a young fellow to sorrow,
>   Who loves this young lady to-day,
>   And loves that young lady to-morrow.

(39)

Of course, were this argument allowed to stand, neither sexual fidelity nor even monogamy could possibly endure: indeed, the Defendant's final proposal is "I'll marry one lady to-day, / And I'll marry the other to-morrow!" (40) Gilbert's view seems to be that, far from being a moral guide, Nature's "authority" is actually a tool that can be self-servingly used to justify nearly any behavior. As Goldberg remarks, "The Defendant's sophistry, and his appeal to Nature . . . are in the finest Rabelaisian tradition; it should be placed beside the Frenchman's *apologia* for drinking: *Natura vacuum abhorret.*"[24]

The characters of the more mature Savoy operas appeal to Nature for similar purposes. In much the same spirit in which Sir Mulberry Hawk asks Kate Nickleby to "be more natural," Mr. Goldbury and Lord Dramaleigh invoke Nature in a lecherous effort to persuade the two demure princesses of *Utopia (Limited)* to loosen up their behavior. And Yum-Yum, in *The Mikado,* finds in it a rationale for her narcissism: "Sometimes I sit and wonder, in my artless Japanese way, why it is that I am so much more attractive than anybody else in the whole world? Can this be vanity? No! Nature is lovely and rejoices in her loveliness. I am a child of Nature, and take after my mother" (251). Vanity, of course, is a mere foible, but Yum-Yum also uses the example of Nature to justify much more serious excesses. Observing the glory of the sun, she sings:

(251)

> I mean to rule the earth,
>   As he the sky—
> We really know our worth,
>   The sun and I!

Such megalomaniacal sentiments would hardly reflect well on anyone expressing them, but Victorians must have found them particularly unbecoming in the mouth of a woman.

Given this evidence of suspicion about the moral reliability of Nature, we should not be surprised that Gilbert infrequently allows it to function as an arbiter of crucial events in the Savoy operas. Rather, Nature's prerogatives, like Providence's, are assigned to human law. In *Ruddigore,* a syllogism deriving from the man-made witch's curse effectively delivers the Murgatroyd family from the mortality that afflicts all Nature's creatures. And in *The Grand Duke,* though human legalities may not negate the natural causes of death, they nevertheless supersede them. As the Notary explains, duels in Pfennig Halbpfennig do not end in biological death; rather, the law allows only for "statutory duels," in which both opponents draw cards, and he who draws the lower dies "*ipso facto,* a social death. He loses all his civil rights—his identity disappears—the Revising Barrister expunges his name from the list of voters, and the winner takes his place, whatever it may be, discharges all his functions and adopts all his responsibilities." (429). However ludicrous it may be to present life and death as functions of law rather than Nature, both these operas show the former effectively arranging the happiness of the sympathetic characters—freeing them from a curse, resurrecting them from the grave, preserving them from the ravages of swords and dueling pistols, and generally ensuring that they survive long enough to collect their rewards in the finales. Here, too, Gilbert's comic dramaturgy responded to the philosophical anxieties of his age.

Still, there are notable instances in which he deviated from the norms of this dramaturgy. Perhaps he was inclined occasionally to experiment; perhaps he was not entirely conscious of his own practices, which may have owed as much to his keen instincts about the marketplace as they did to deliberate choice. Whatever the causes, we find among the high Savoy series such anomalies as the traditionally structured law-to-liberty plot of *The Yeomen of the Guard,* the conspicuous absence of benignity among the ostensibly sympathetic characters of *Ruddigore,* and the unblushing endorsement of Nature's dictates in *Princess Ida.* Each of the next three sections of this chapter will, respectively, discuss the details and the results of each of these detours from Gilbert's established comedic path.

Gilbert did not decisively mark this path as his own, however, until *H.M.S. Pinafore* (1878). As previously observed, *Thespis* (1871), *Trial By Jury* (1875), and *The Sorcerer* (1877) remained substantially traditional and anti-legal in their content; they also remained limited in their audience appeal. That *Pinafore* was not only the first great success of the collaboration but also the first of the operas to be based upon what was to become the standard comedic formula of the Savoy series seems far from coincidental.

The importance of *Pinafore* as a watershed in Gilbert's career is generally acknowledged. Jessie Bond, who joined D'Oyly Carte's company at the time of this opera's premiere, recalled in her memoirs that "it was then that Gilbert and Sullivan opera first became really popular. *Trial By Jury* and *The Sorcerer* had just given discerning hearers a hint of what to expect, but they had never of themselves gripped the public." And Thorndike bluntly states that "If Gilbert had died before *Pinafore* was produced, he would not deserve much attention in a history of English comedy."[25] The remainder of this chapter will explore the dramaturgical principles that informed *Pinafore* and its successors, and that earned their author not only the attention of history but the adulation of his own age.

Law and Plot

The originality of Gilbert's comedic plot-making consisted in the inevitability of his endings. Once the crucial law of each opera is announced, the remainder of the plot becomes the story not of *whether* but rather of *how* this law is to be fulfilled.

Starting with law was not, of course, a Gilbertian innovation. Indeed, Frye comments on "how often the action of a Shakespearean comedy begins with some absurd, cruel, or irrational law; the law of killing Syracusans in the *Comedy of Errors,* the law of compulsory marriage in *A Midsummer Night's Dream,* the law that confirms Shylock's bond, the attempts of Angelo to legislate people into righteousness, and the like, which the action of a comedy evades or breaks."[26] But though Gilbert likewise sets his plots in motion by means of problematic laws, the action of his Savoy comedies neither evades nor breaks them. Rather, happy endings are achieved when the characters finally find themselves able and willing to offer obedience. All the operas from *Pinafore* on, except *The Yeomen of the Guard,* follow this pattern:

In *Pinafore,* the problematic law is articulated by Dick Deadeye to the lovelorn sailor Ralph: "captains' daughters don't marry foremast jacks" (83)—that is, lovers should seek their mates in their own social stations. But once the true identities of Ralph and the Captain have been sorted out and it is ascertained who really belongs to which social rank, the Captain is able to wed his beloved without violating this law, and Ralph receives a special dispensation from Sir Joseph—the law's chief representative aboard Her Majesty's ship—to do the same.

In *The Pirates of Penzance,* the more general notion that one must always do one's duty creates the initial conflict, as Frederic interprets it to mean that he must exterminate his pirate comrades as soon as he has left their band. But once these buccaneers come to see where their own duty truly lies, their obedience to this same notion sets the plot right: they obey the Sergeant's charge to surrender themselves as soon as his invocation of Queen Victoria's name reminds them of their duty as British subjects, and they presumably obey the Major-General when he learns that they are actually peers and calls upon them to "Resume your ranks and legislative duties, / And take my daughters, all of whom are beauties" (134).

In *Patience,* the exposition ends and the action truly begins after Lady Angela tells the title character that "Love that is tainted with selfishness is no love" (152). But though this principle at first prevents Patience from loving Grosvenor, the perfect aesthetic poet whom she longs for, it ultimately permits her to marry him, once Grosvenor has been forced by Bunthorne to assume the imperfections of a commonplace young man.

In *Iolanthe,* the law that has caused the title character's past problems stipulates that "every fairy must die who marries a mortal" (201). It is implicitly reasserted as the opera's action begins, for the Fairy Queen effects Iolanthe's freedom not by repealing this law but rather by pardoning her violation of it. Later, when the Lord Chancellor persuades the Queen to change it to "every fairy shall die who *don't* marry a mortal" and thus to sanction the happy union of all the characters with their chosen mates, the law is still not discarded; rather, it is retained and amended, however radically, by "the insertion of a single word" (201).

In *Princess Ida* and *The Gondoliers,* the law that creates the initial difficulties is represented by the contract binding each heroine to a man whom she married in infancy. But while Ida first spurns this bond, she achieves love and joy when persuaded at last to honor it. Casilda, initially, is no happier than Ida about her legal obligation, which requires her to renounce her beloved Luiz and vow fidelity to a husband whom nobody can identify—but her obligation becomes a delight when she learns in the finale that Luiz and this husband are one and the same.

In *The Mikado,* Ko-Ko's troubles begin when the emperor decrees that an execution must take place. And, though no blood is ever actually shed, the plot is fully resolved only when Ko-Ko's faulty syllogism proves to the monarch that his decree has been fulfilled.

In *Ruddigore,* the miseries of the Murgatroyds in general and Robin in particular spring from the witch's curse requiring each baronet to commit a daily crime. But the happy ending springs, not from defying this "law," but rather from Robin's apparently logical demonstration that all his ancestors have actually fulfilled it.

In *Utopia (Limited),* when King Paramount determines to bring English laws and customs to his island nation, he puts himself in perilous conflict with the powerful and self-serving wise men, who wish to maintain the old Utopian ways. When these imported laws are triumphantly preserved by the climactic addition of "Government by Party" (412), the wise men's attempt to overturn the new order is thwarted, while Paramount secures his throne and wins a bride.

And, in *The Grand Duke,* the law is initially a problem inasmuch as it is embodied in an obnoxious autocrat whom the sympathetic characters plot to overthrow. However, when Ludwig actually replaces Rudolph as grand duke, he discovers that he has also inherited contractual obligations to marry three different women and must, consequently, renounce his beloved Lisa. Only the lawful monarch's restoration to power effectively and happily disentangles the various romantic problems knotted during the interregnum. Significantly, this restoration is effected by the full and fair application of the same statute that was less honestly and accurately used to remove him from his throne.

Ellis aptly summarizes this pattern: "The Gilbertian ending not only depends upon a reapplication of the same logic which initiated the conflict, but in a single stroke metes out rewards and punishments, decides the inevitable marriages, and upholds the principles behind the action."[27]

And the thrust of this "logic" is diametrically opposed to that of traditional comedy. Frye holds that, in the latter, "The society emerging at the conclusion of comedy represents . . . a kind of moral norm, or pragmatically free society. Its ideals are seldom defined or formulated; definition and formulation belong to the humors, who want predictable activity. We are simply given to understand that the newly married couple will live happily ever after, or that at any rate they will get along in a relatively unhumorous and clear-sighted manner." In the typical traditional ending, "the device in the plot that brings hero and heroine together causes a new society to crystallize around the hero,"[28] who represents, for his fellow characters, the "moral norm" of this "free society." He thus becomes the exemplar from whom the others can inductively draw conclusions about how they too should live. But in Gilbert's mature comedy, the laws of conduct *are* fully "defined" and "formulated," and the hero, like the other characters, must obediently apply these generalizations to his specific circumstances if he wishes to win happiness. In short, the new societies that crystallize in the Savoy denouements are deductively achieved.

Here we return to Gilbert's predilection for syllogisms. As the initially problematic law, or major premise, of each plot is normally established at or near the beginning of each opera's action, the whole point of that action frequently becomes the search for the proper minor premise, which likewise proves to have the force of law behind it. *Patience* presents a typical case. Angela tells the title character: "Love that is tainted with selfishness is no love. Oh, try, try, try to love!" (152) Patience interprets this to mean that love is a "duty" (159, 160), thus granting the major premise the force of law. She also determines that truly unselfish love must fasten upon an imperfect object: consequently, the perfectly beautiful Grosvenor is unfit for her affections, which are bestowed instead on the bilious and bad-tempered Bunthorne. Indeed, the song in which Patience explains her love for Bunthorne is cast in explicitly syllogistic form, beginning with a restatement of the major premise taught her by Angela ("True love must single-hearted be— / . . . From every selfish fancy free"), and moving on to a minor premise and conclusion about Bunthorne ("It follows then, a maiden who / Devotes herself to loving *you* / . . . Is prompted by no selfish view" [156]). But Bunthorne is not content with the love of only Patience, for he is consumed with jealousy when he sees the Rapturous Maidens transfer to Grosvenor the adoration that was once his. Cleverly, he decides to threaten his susceptible rival with a curse unless that rival will consent to transform himself into an unattractive and commonplace young man—and the plan works, as Grosvenor submissively makes the changes demanded of him ("I do it on compulsion" [165]). However, Bunthorne's ingenuity backfires: Grosvenor's transformation now qualifies him as a candidate for Patience's unselfish love, while Bunthorne's declared resolution to perfect himself has the opposite effect. Patience is now able to apply to Grosvenor the same minor premise that she previously applied to Bunthorne, and—given that she regards unselfish love as a duty— the happy ending becomes inevitable.

Rationalization supplies some minor premises. In *Ruddigore,* for instance, Robin ingeniously discovers that a provision of the criminal code (the law against suicide) may serve as the crux of an argument which proves that he and his ancestors have actually fulfilled the witch's curse which is the major premise. And, in *Princess Ida,* Hildebrand makes shrewd use of biological law in his critique of Ida's sexual isolation—which, he points out, will ultimately render impossible the "Posterity" to which she hopes to pass on her "scheme"—and thus persuades her to "see my error" and accept "with joy" the legal contract that has bound her to Hilarion from the start (234, 235). Revelations of identity supply other minor premises, as witnesses testify that Ralph and the Captain in *Pinafore,* the title characters in *The Pirates of Penzance,* and Luiz in *The Gondoliers* are all, legally, other than who they seem. In all of these operas, the invention or discovery of the minor premise represents the climax of the plot, for each such act proves decisive in enabling the characters happily to obey the laws embodied in the previously established major premises.

In other operas, in the legalistic spirit of judicial review and legislative amendment, the same result is achieved through last-minute adjustments to the major premises. Having secured domestic tranquility by enacting three Reform Bills during a half-century in which revolution convulsed much of the rest of Europe, the late Victorians would have considered one of the prime virtues of their political system to consist in its susceptibility to just such adjustment: as one could replace the parts of one of the machines behind Britain's recent economic growth without discarding the machine itself, so the non-functional or outmoded parts of the law could be replaced or repaired without destruction of the entire system. Thus, *Iolanthe*—produced just two years before the passage of the Third Reform Bill—has its major premise supplemented by one extra word, that of *Utopia (Limited)* (expressed in the royal decree "That all Utopia shall henceforth be modelled / Upon that glorious country called Great Britain" [388]) is modified only by the addition of Government by Party; and the law in *The Grand Duke* on statutory duels is revised to reflect the Notary's discovery that, according to the rules, "Ace shall invariably count as lowest" (451). But no major premise is ever abandoned, and once the necessary adjustments (if any) have been made to it, it combines with whatever minor premise has emerged from the action to produce the happy ending. And this ending now follows as inevitably as does the conclusion from the two premises of a syllogism. Mill, to be sure, takes pains to qualify the absoluteness of this concept: while nodding to the conventional wisdom that, in syllogisms, "if the premises are true, the conclusions must inevitably be so," he adds that "The only sense in which necessity can be ascribed to the conclusions of any scientific investigation, is that of legitimately following from some assumption, which, by the conditions of the inquiry, is not to be questioned."[29] But Gilbert's characters raise no troublesome questions; rather, they passively grant axiomatic status to the premises thrust upon them and are thus positioned to hail as necessary the agreeable conclusions derived therefrom—however ironically their reasoning may be regarded by a more empirically inclined audience.

To the same extent that the foregoing analysis may explain what Gilbert's mature plots are, it also defines what traditional comedic plots are not. In the latter, Frye notes that "The drive toward a comic conclusion is so powerful that it breaks all the chains of probability in the plot"; consequently, "what emerges in the end is not a logical consequence of the preceding action, as in tragedy, but something more like a metamorphosis." Thus:

> *In striking contrast to tragedy, there can hardly be such a thing as an inevitable comedy, as far as the action of the individual play is concerned. That is, we may know that the convention of comedy will make some kind of happy ending inevitable, but still for each play the dramatist must produce a distinctive "gimmick" or "weenie," to use two disrespectful Hollywood synonyms for anagnorisis. Happy endings do not impress us as true, but as desirable, and they are brought about by manipulation. . . . Civilizations which stress the desirable rather than the real, and the religious as opposed to the scientific perspective, think of drama almost entirely in terms of comedy.[30]*

Among nineteenth-century playwrights, the melodramatists, with their *deus ex machina* endings, and the pantomimists, with their all-resolving transformation scenes, were most conspicuously given to constructing such plots, but the practitioners of all the standard comedic genres did the same. Some adapted the traditional approach with skill and even subtlety, but theirs proved to be the right product in the wrong age. Gilbert, on the other hand, was sensitive to the intellectual prejudices of his era's ascendant class, prejudices which favored the pragmatic advances of applied science just as much as they feared the philosophical depradations of scientific theory. He therefore chose to base his plots upon the same deductive method that contemporary inventors and engineers used to devise specific applications (or minor premises) for the general laws of science (or major premises) and so to attain the manifold blessings of progress. Much of Gilbert's bourgeois audience owed their rise on the social scale to the technological triumphs achieved since the onset of the Industrial Revolution; they thus felt little ambivalence about the value of such progress, and the civilization they dominated was, accordingly, one that stressed the real rather than the desirable. In an era increasingly doubtful about the promises of religion but empirically convinced of the beneficence of science, Gilbert constructed plots in which miraculous metamorphoses were displaced by syllogistic progressions toward inevitable conclusions.

And, just as the laws applied by scientists had freed the Victorians from many restraints of Nature, so the laws affirmed and enforced by the high Savoy plots liberate the characters from various forms of bondage. In the finales to the operas, we see Ralph freed from his dungeon cell in *Pinafore,* the pirates from the custody of the police (and Frederic from his service to the pirates), Patience from her miserable engagement to Bunthorne, all the fairies in *Iolanthe* from the threat of execution, Princess Ida and her students from the "Castle Adamant" in which she had confined herself and them, Ko-Ko and his accomplices from the Mikado's sentence of death, the past baronets of Ruddigore from actual death (and Robin from the present requirements of the witch's curse), the various lovers of *The Gondoliers* from undesired marital obligations and restraints, King Paramount once and for all from the control of the wise men, and the legal ghosts of *The Grand Duke* from their legal graves. In every one of these instances, the achievement of freedom is made possible not *in spite of* but rather *because of* law. And we may further understand that the characters will only continue to enjoy their freedom as long as they remain *under* the laws of their respective major premises, which are as much in force at each curtain's fall as they were at its rise. Again, there is an analogy in the new physical freedoms enabled by science, which would likewise have vanished if natural laws ceased to function: steam locomotives would no longer have permitted the rapid conquest of distance if water no longer boiled at a fixed temperature.

Ironically, the dramatic vehicle which Gilbert frequently uses to convey the law's ultimate triumph is the transformation scene, adapted from pantomime and extravaganza, those most radically anti-legal genres of nineteenth-century comedy. But Gilbert's characters are subject only to such metamorphoses as are prompted or even required by the law. Thus, the noblemen in *Iolanthe* become fairies in response to the legislation throwing the peerage open to attainment by Competitive Examination ("Well, now that the Peers are to be recruited entirely from persons of intelligence," says Lord Mountararat, "I really don't see what use *we* are, down here" [202]), while the past baronets of *Ruddigore* are compelled to a change from death to life by the force of Robin's legalistic reinterpretation of the witch's curse. But the most interesting and significant of the Savoy transformations are those we see in the denouements of *The Pirates of Penzance* (in which the pirates become peers), *Patience* (in which the aesthetic maidens become everyday young girls, emulating Grosvenor's transformation into a commonplace young man), *Princess Ida* (in which Ida, Psyche, Melissa, and possibly others among the students of Castle Adamant elect to become domesticated young women), *The Gondoliers* (in which the kings and their courtiers resume their identities as *gondolieri*), and *The Grand Duke* (in which the sometime duke Ludwig and his mock-Grecian courtiers revert to their calling as actors). Each of these entirely reverses the pattern of the transformations found in pantomime and extravaganza, as Gilbert moves his characters from some fanciful, exotic, or otherwise unlikely plane of existence to one which is much more mundane and realistically restricted, thus crowning the assertion of law that is the thrust of each piece's action. A similarly conceived transformation also occurs, though much more gradually, in *Utopia (Limited)*, as the colorfully primitive South Sea Islanders are taught to become replicas of ordinary nineteenth-century Britons.

Melodrama, too, furnished Gilbert some points for his high Savoy plots.[31] It was undoubtably from the melodramatists that he inherited the habit of placing his sympathetic characters in dire peril at the penultimate point in most of the operas: thus we find characters threatened with death just before the resolutions of *Iolanthe, The Mikado,* and *Ruddigore;* with imprisonment in *Pinafore* and *The Pirates of Penzance;* and with revolution in *Utopia (Limited).* As in melodrama, they are rescued from disaster by a benevolent power that has brooded over the action from the start and is triumphantly vindicated at the finish. The difference between the two kinds of comedy has to do, of course, with the identity of this power: what Providence does in melodrama's plots, a man-made major premise does in Gilbert's. And the difference was crucially important to the greater favor Gilbert's comedy found among the religiously skeptical audiences of the century's final decades.

Perhaps the most significant indication of Gilbert's dissent from melodrama's creed is found in the very different value and plot function that he assigned to conscience. As long as religious certainty had persisted, the moral authority of conscience—God's surrogate in each human breast—remained unchallenged. Thus, given the theistic presumptions of the genre, it is not surprising that "the heart or conscience of a good man is, in melodrama, always to be trusted. . . . usually the instigations of these hearts were considered an almost sacred duty."[32] Indeed, conscience seems to retain its moral reliability even when at work within a bad man: it moves the villainous Captain Crosstree to save William's life in Jerrold's *Black-Ey'd Susan* (1829); it afflicts the monstrous title character of C. H. Hazlewood's *Lady Audley's Secret* (1863) with a mortally guilty madness; and it tries, convicts, and executes the murderer Mathias in Leopold Lewis's *The Bells* (1871). In each of these instances, its promptings remain ethically perfect—for it leads the affected individuals either to do justice or to have justice done upon them—and its role in determining the outcome of the plot is crucial.

However, as conscience inevitably became detached from God in the post-theistic perceptions of the late Victorian era, its dictates were stripped of their automatic validity. And Gilbert clearly had doubts about its reliability from the earliest years of his career. An 1869 Bab ballad entitled "Hongree and Mahry: A Richardsonian Melodrama"[33] reflects his suspicion about the convenience with which private conviction may operate. In this poem, "HONGREE, Sub-Lieutenant of Chassoores" in the French forces of the Hundred Years War, loves and is beloved by Mahry, who is also the object of Lieutenant Colonel Jooles's desire. Jooles attempts to eliminate his rival by ordering Hongree to lead 20 men in attacking the 2,000 in the English camp, but Hongree now discovers that his conscience forbids him to obey. Instead, he goes to the Duke of Bedford, the English commander, and tells him:

> My colonel will attack your camp to-night,
> And orders me to lead the hope forlorn.
> Now I am sure our excellent KING CHARLES
> Would not approve of this; but he's away
> A hundred leagues, and rather more than that.
> So, utterly devoted to my King,
> Blinded by my attachment to the throne,
> And having but its interest at heart,
> I feel it is my duty to disclose
> All schemes that emanate from COLONEL JOOLES,
> If I believe that they are not the kind
> Of schemes that our good monarch could approve.

He then leads the English "by a secret path / Into the heart of COLONEL JOOLES' array" so that they can "attack them unprepared, / And slay my fellow-countrymen unarmed." Having thus discharged the duty that his delicately selective conscience holds honorable, Hongree receives Mahry's hand as a token of the Duke's gratitude. The plot, then, rewards his actions, but the massive slaughter of innocents that these actions produce makes it difficult to regard him as a sympathetic character and impossible to miss the irony of Gilbert's perspective.

Eighteen years later, we find Hongree reincarnated in a different branch of the service, as he has now metamorphosed into Dick Dauntless, *Ruddigore*'s spoof upon that stock figure of nineteenth-century melodrama, the noble British tar. Like Hongree, Dick unhesitatingly trusts his inner promptings—"Let your heart be your compass," he says, "with a clear conscience for your binnacle light, and you'll sail ten knots on a bowline, clear of shoals, rocks, and quicksands!" (283)—and, like Hongree's, Dick's conveniently calibrated moral instrument points him exclusively in the direction of his self-advantage. Though Dick has for years possessed the secret that his foster brother Robin is only posing as a farmer and is in reality heir to the baronetcy of Ruddigore and its concomitant witch's curse, he feels compelled by conscience to reveal this secret only when he finds himself competing with Robin for the affections of respectable Rose Maybud. But Gilbert did not allow conscience to play the same decisive role in his mature Savoy plot as it had in his early Bab ballad; rather, it is superseded by the law enforced in the opera's resolution, which enables Robin to reclaim Rose and residually consigns Dick to the first lady of the chorus. Frederic's conscience is similarly, and fortunately, overruled in *The Pirates of Penzance*. Left to his private moral devices and unaware that his former comrades are all noblemen in disguise, the ex-pirate apprentice determines to direct the wholesale murder of the buccaneers. Only the Pirate King's insistence that Frederic fulfill his articles of indenture saves him from doing this terrible deed.

It is significant that the King saves Frederic from himself by insisting on "the letter of your bond," which requires the apprentice to serve the pirates "until . . . your twenty-first birthday" (128)—a milestone which a lad born on February 29 does not attain until his eighty-fourth year. Unlike the dictates of conscience, the letter of the law can be objectively confirmed, and this may be why it emerges in Gilbert's comedy as the most morally reliable arbiter of his plots. Stedman remarks upon how frequently "The state of life or death is dependent on a word; quibble, lip-service, or nomenclature usurps the law of nature. The moral foundation of legality gives way to the letter of the law."[34] The new dispensation may have lacked the ethical grandeur of divinely dispensed morality, but it compensated with the empirical verifiability particularly valued by a scientific age. And it is as beneficent to the high Savoy characters as ever God could be.

Indeed, in those plots in which a distinction is made between the two, the spirit killeth and the letter giveth life. In *Pinafore* and *The Pirates of Penzance,* birth certificates take precedence over past and present merits and demerits in determining the identities and deciding the fates of Ralph, Captain Corcoran, and the pirate band; the result is that all these characters get brides instead of prison terms. Similarly, when Ko-Ko sophistically persuades the Mikado to accept a certificate of death in full satisfaction of the royal demand for an execution, the spirit of the monarch's decree is entirely, and happily, subverted. And though a similarly fatal spirit informs both the fairy law of *Iolanthe* and the witch's curse of *Ruddigore,* amendment of the former and reinterpretation of the latter enable the characters to achieve life and even resurrection by obeying the literal sense of each.

But in one high Savoy opera, the law does not come to the aid of the sympathetic characters. In *The Yeomen of the Guard,* we find the only plot in the series that is based upon the law-to-liberty pattern of traditional comedy. As such, it provided Gilbert an opportunity to demonstrate the injustice inherent in the plots of such comedy; for us, it provides the exception that proves the rules of the other Savoy plots.

The story concerns Colonel Fairfax, who has been unjustly sentenced to die in the Tower of London. An evil kinsman has falsely accused him of sorcery and hopes thus to inherit Fairfax's fortune, but the condemned man determines to foil this scheme by marrying in his final hour and so diverting his estate to another beneficiary. Unconcerned about whom he marries, he asks the Lieutenant of the Tower to bring him any willing girl, and the Lieutenant soon lights upon Elsie, a strolling minstrel who needs money to buy medicine for her sick mother. Elsie and Jack Point, her partner and aspiring lover, consent to the marriage on the understanding that it will be of very brief duration; the girl is then led blindfolded to Fairfax's cell. But shortly afterward, the colonel is helped to escape by Sergeant Meryll and his daughter Phoebe.

The fugitive now disguises himself as Leonard Meryll, the sergeant's son, while Elsie laments having bound herself permanently to an unknown husband. Point is no happier about the turn events have taken and, wishing to marry Elsie himself, misleads her into believing that Fairfax has been hunted down and killed. But the supposed Leonard steps in ahead of Point, maintaining his disguise as he woos and wins the love of his own wife. A royal reprieve now arrives for Fairfax, and he resumes his proper person. But as Elsie rejoices to learn that her beloved "Leonard" and her husband are actually one and the same, the heartbroken Point falls dead at the young couple's feet.[35]

The death of Point has misled some critics into calling the opera a tragedy. But Frye rightly objects to the indiscriminate use of this label, holding that "The death of a central character" such as Little Nell in *The Old Curiosity Shop,* "does not make a story tragic, any more than a similar device does in *The King and I* or *The Yeomen of the Guard.*"[36] For, he asserts, "A comedy is not a play which ends happily: it is a play in which a certain structure is present and works through to its own logical end."[37]

The structure of traditional comedy is certainly present in *The Yeomen of the Guard.* The movement toward resolution of its plot depends absolutely upon defiance of the law: if Fairfax has not been enabled to escape from prison when he did, his execution would have taken place on schedule during the first-act finale, and the fact that a reprieve later sanctions his freedom would have been irrelevant. And the resolution in question is as comedically traditional as the anti-legal means that make it possible: the tenor and soprano are securely united as the hero is finally and fully freed from the menace of law. Indeed, the action of the opera drives so unrelentingly toward this joyful romantic conclusion that it crushes anyone who stands in its way. The primary victim is Jack Point, who refuses to bless the final festivities: "Oh thoughtless crew!" he sings to the revelers who join in the present happiness of Fairfax and Elsie, "Ye know not what ye do!" (338) His removal is necessary to their future happiness, which would surely be blighted were this jilted former lover of the bride to continue moping reproachfully around them.

Nor is Point the only sympathetic character whom the plot rolls over. Law is not to be mocked in Gilbert's mature comedy, and if hero and heroine are enabled to achieve their happiness as a result of defiance of law, those who initiated this defiance must pay the price. The debt falls due to Sergeant Meryll and Phoebe, the prime movers in the plot to free the relatively passive Fairfax from prison. Father and daughter are blackmailed into marriage by suitors they have formerly scorned, Dame Carruthers and Wilfred Shadbolt, who have learned of the legally culpable part that the Merylls played in the hero's escape. By stepping outside the law, they expose themselves to misery.

Point, likewise, first gets himself into trouble when he is persuaded to flout the laws he normally lives by. When the Lieutenant offers Elsie 100 crowns to become Fairfax's bride for an hour, Point responds:

> Though as a general rule of life
> I don't allow my promised wife,
> My lovely bride that is to be,
> To marry anyone but me,
>   The circumstances
>   Of this case
>   May set such fancies
>   Out of place;
> So, if the fee is duly paid,
> And he, in well-earned grave,
> Within the hour is duly laid,
> Objection I will waive!

(322)

Given the unexpected consequences that follow for Point from Elsie's marriage and her bridegroom's subsequent escape, we see clearly by the end of the play that the abandoned jester should have rigidly adhered to his "general rule of life."

Point's unintentionally decisive role in thrusting Elsie into the arms of Fairfax makes it fitting that he should pay the law an even heavier toll than the Merylls incur for starting the lovers along the path to liberty. That he dies on their account is suggested by the final stage direction, which specifies that "Fairfax embraces Elsie as

Point falls insensible at their feet" (339). Nothing less than his death can clear this account, for only a life will satisfy the law. Phoebe recognizes this early in the play, as she laments Fairfax's prospective fate and curses at "this wicked Tower" which "like a cruel giant in a fairy tale, must be fed with blood, and that blood must be the best and bravest in England, or it's not good enough for the old Blunderbore" (317). But Fairfax's blood is not to be had, and the Tower proves less fastidious than Phoebe supposes, accepting Point as a substitute, even though he himself admits that he is hardly "a brave man" (335). And it is precisely the lack of spiritual stature in its victim that differentiates *Yeomen* from tragedy: Point's fall is not "the fall of a great man," says Diana C. Burleigh, who rightly holds that his "only flaw seems to be that he loved a pretty young girl."[38]

But if the jester does not qualify as a tragic hero, he may be assigned to another class of character. Charney notes that "The theory and practice of the ritual clown is well documented from the study of various Indian tribes of the Southwest, especially the Zuñi Katcinas. The annual appointment of a ritual clown provides an ingenious safety valve for the pressures, guilts, and accumulated repressions of the society."[39] And Charney further observes that this figure may be compared to the scapegoat, for his function is publicly to enact society's taboos and thus draw the anger of the gods toward him and away from the community. Gilbert may have conceived Point, a jester by trade, as a comic scapegoat who unwillingly and unknowingly diverts to himself the fury of offended law and thus allows the lovers to live in unmolested liberty. Like the ritual clown, he places himself directly in the line of fire. He deceives Elsie into thinking Fairfax dead as a first step toward persuading her to marry him and so become an unwitting bigamist; he is thus responsible for at least attempting to enact one of society's most serious taboos. But this anti-legal initiative backfires in the same direction as did his earlier suspension of his "general rule of life." Both, ironically, help to bring Elsie and Fairfax together: without Point's consent she would never have married in the first place, and without believing herself to be a widow, she would never have listened to the addresses of the supposed Leonard and so learned to love him. If the law must be appeased for losing Fairfax to Elsie, we can understand why Point, an official clown who defies social taboo, should become the scapegoat.

We understand, but we do not cheer. For the sacrificial victim in any ritual of vicarious atonement must always seem to us unfairly dealt with, and to the extent we perceive Point's death as payment for Fairfax's escape, he claims the protest of our pity. Indeed, our sense of injustice is intensified when we recall that he first bypasses law out of the noblest of motives, consenting to Elsie's marriage only because the "fee" the Lieutenant offers will enable her to buy medicine for her sickly mother. Nor are the Merylls any less unselfish in their motives for effecting Fairfax's escape: the sergeant wishes to repay the debt of life that he owes to his former comrade-in-arms, while Phoebe worships him from afar as "the bravest, the handsomest, and the best young gentleman in England," who "twice saved my father's life" (317). Just as we pity Point, we likewise are saddened by the unhappy consequences that father and daughter reap from their actions, for we feel that they deserve better.

But I believe that the fates of all three characters are intended to make a point: those who go beyond the pale of law take themselves, *ipso facto,* beyond the pale of justice. Gilbert's libretto concedes that human law is far from perfect in its doings—it has, after all, temporarily been manipulated into sanctioning the execution of the innocent Fairfax—but it nonetheless embodies the most reliable set of objective ethical standards left to post-theistic society. As the action of traditional comedy casts these standards aside in its purposive drive toward the happiness of its young lovers, such comedy must, in Gilbert's view, have been as likely as not to arrive at conclusions that are unjust and unhappy for all but these lovers. Thus, I would suggest that if the ending of *The Yeomen of the Guard* elicits more tears than smiles, this happens not because it is a tragedy but rather because, for once in the high Savoy series, Gilbert gave his audiences a traditional comedy.

Still, if the non-traditional dramaturgy of this series had been primarily responsible for winning and retaining the loyalty of these audiences, why did they so highly favor *The Yeomen of the Guard*?

One answer is suggested by the foregoing discussion: though the comic action may follow a traditional law-to-liberty pattern, it nevertheless affirmed bourgeois values by offering a negative demonstration of the desirability of obedience to law. Moreover, the play's Tudor setting and trappings may successfully have borrowed for it the respectability that polite Victorian audiences conceded to antiquarian productions of Shakespeare's comedies. Gilbert, indeed, took great pains to ensure the period accuracy of the sets and costumes,[40] and the content of the script distinguishes it from such other high Savoy operas as *Princess Ida* and *The Grand Duke,* in which anachronism undercuts the effect of chronological distancing: in *Yeomen,* not an allusion is made nor a word spoken which could not conceivably have passed through sixteenth-century lips, and the diction of the dialogue is deliberately littered with archaisms in a somewhat strained attempt to evoke a Renaissance atmosphere. At any rate, whatever the impact of its historical authenticity, *Yeomen* achieved an initial run of 423 performances, a moderate success even by the inflated standards that the Gilbert and Sullivan partnership had by then established for itself.

Nonetheless, Gilbert felt uneasy about continuing along the same lines, and when the new opera was not yet five months into its run, he wrote to Sullivan:

> *The success of* The Yeomen, *which is a stage in the direction of serious opera, has not been so convincing as to warrant us in assuming that the public wants something more earnest still. There is no doubt about it that the more reckless and irresponsible the libretto has been, the better the piece has succeeded. The pieces that have succeeded least have been those in which a consistent story has been more or less consistently followed out. Personally, I prefer a consistent subject. Such a subject as* The Yeomen *is far more congenial to my taste than the burlesquerie of* Iolanthe *or* The Mikado, *but I think we should be risking everything in writing more seriously still. We have a name jointly for humorous work tempered with occasional glimpses of earnest drama. I think we should do unwisely if we left altogether the path we have trodden together so long and so successfully.*[41]

It is not clear exactly why Gilbert considered *Yeomen* "a consistent story . . . consistently followed out": its consistency is certainly not that of plot, for, as Audrey Williamson has pointed out, the sequence of the scenes is chronologically impossible, and events occur (such as the arrest of Wilfred at the end of the first act) without their logical sequels (as we find Wilfred inexplicably free at the start of the second act).[42] Rather, I believe he was thinking of comedy in which the tendencies of the characters' personalities are "consistently followed out" and in which no higher power, be it Providence or law, intervenes either to guide their choices or to save them from the consequences thereof. Such comedy is obviously closer to reality, but Gilbert apparently knew that his public preferred the "reckless and irresponsible" spectacle of a beneficently regulated comedic universe. And this is precisely what he gave them in the successor to *Yeomen*. *The Gondoliers* features the familiar Savoy pattern, in which the various pieces of the happy ending fall into place once the legal tie binding Casilda to Luiz is discovered and asserted. The enthusiasm with which the reviewer of the *Illustrated London News* greeted its premiere had much to do with its familiarity: "Mr. W. S. Gilbert has returned to the Gilbert of the past, and everyone is delighted. He is himself again . . . the Gilbert of whimsical conceit, inoffensive cynicism, subtle satire, and playful paradox; the Gilbert who invented a school of his own . . . that is the Gilbert the public want to see, and this is the Gilbert who on Saturday night was cheered till the audience was weary of cheering any more."[43] And this was also the Gilbert of the pro-legal, non-traditional comic plot—the Gilbert who made himself rich by giving this public exactly what it wanted.

Law and Character

If the Victorian middle classes were philosophically uncomfortable with the plot pattern of traditional comedy, they were emotionally repelled by its characterization. In the year before the premiere of *Pinafore,* George Meredith described their attitude:

> *Of this class in England, a large body, neither Puritan nor Bacchanalian, have a sentimental objection to face the study of the*

> *actual world. . . . of comedy they have a shivering dread, for*
> *comedy enfolds them with the wretched host of the world, huddles*
> *them with us all in an ignoble assimilation, and cannot be used by*
> *any exalted variety as a scourge and a broom. . . . You may*
> *distinguish them by a favorite phrase: "Surely we are not so bad!"*
> *and the remark: "If that is human nature, save us from it!"*[44]

This lesson in audience taste cost Gilbert some pains to learn. In the year that Meredith's essay was published, Gilbert produced *Engaged* at the Haymarket; though it may well have been the best play he ever wrote, it lasted a mere 105 performances. The public's objections, as one reviewer after another made clear, focused on the author's "cynical" approach to characterization. Typical of the critical response were the fulminations of the *Figaro:*

> *The hero is a combination of mental imbecility, vulgar cunning,*
> *paltry mendacity, greedy stinginess, shameless cowardice, and*
> *unctuous sensuality. A Scotch peasant girl is introduced, with her*
> *betrothed, of whom the hero buys her for two pounds, in conse-*
> *quence of her own graceful intercession; her betrothed is delighted*
> *with the bargain, and complacently looks on while the purchaser*
> *caresses his modest acquisition. Later in the piece, this girl's*
> *mother approves the contract, and when her daughter has changed*
> *her mind offers to supply her place. There are two other young*
> *girls introduced, who vie with one another in the sentimental*
> *utterance of such mercenary principles as the most degraded woman*
> *might possibly feel, but would be ashamed to confess. From begin-*
> *ning to end of this nauseous play not one of the characters ever says*
> *a single word or does a single action that is not inseparable from the*
> *lowest moral degradation.*[45]

Meanwhile, across town at the Vaudeville, H. J. Byron's *Our Boys* was approaching its third anniversary; it was eventually to run almost four and one-half years, achieving an unprecedented 1,362 performances in the process. Byron had been a mentor to Gilbert in the early days of the latter's career—as editor of *Fun* in the sixties, he had cultivated the budding author of the Bab ballads—and with *Our Boys* he showed that he still had some useful lessons to teach.

Its success was founded upon its appeal to middle-class sensibilities: by far the most popular of its characters was the "good-hearted Middlewick," a retired bourgeois butterman who attempts to play the *senex iratus* when his son defies his wishes but who melts in tenderness and sympathy when he later finds his boy living in reduced circumstances. Indeed, the title of the play emphasizes the benevolent affection felt both by Middlewick and Sir Geoffry Champneys for their rebellious offspring; still, as Jim Davis writes, "In demonstrating that a successful middle-class tradesman was as good as any haughty aristocrat Byron appealed directly to the complacency of the middle-class theatre-going public."[46] But each of the fathers is cast in the kindliest of lights by the closing lines Sir Geoffry speaks on behalf of both:

> *We haven't understood each other, borne with each other, we haven't shown sufficient of the glorious old principle of "Give and take." Sister, boys and girls, old friend, (to Middlewick) hot tempers, hasty judgements, extreme crotchets, thick-skinned prejudice, theory and rule run rampant, ignoring the imperfections of poor human nature—these henceforth, we throw overboard and rise to brighter realms, even as the aspiring aeronaut flings away his heavy ballast and floats serenely through the cloudless sky. (Melody in orchestra swells as curtain falls on picture.)*[47]

The most rabid sentimentalist in a Victorian audience could hardly have asked for more.

This sentimental bourgeois preference for the representation of benevolence on the stage continued unabated through most of the high Savoy era. It was again given voice in 1888 by Clement Scott, spokesman for "the great mass of stolid, respectable, middle-class opinion," when he wrote, "I can see no value in a play that only provokes disgust—no pity, no love, no charity, no mercy, no tenderness, no nobility—only cowardice, meanness, and horror."[48] And it was ultimately noted and respected by Gilbert, who achieved most of his greatest successes during the decade bounded by Meredith's and Scott's remarks.

"If they want insipidity," exclaims Bunthorne of the aesthetic maidens in *Patience,* "they shall have it" (160). Gilbert might have said nearly the same about his public. His characters, A. H. Godwin observes, are "almost exasperatingly pleasant," endowed only with "harmless foibles and amiable weaknesses"; "taking them all in all," they "are righteous and orderly people . . . as Victorian as the Victorian who created them." To some extent, the benignity of these people may merely have been the inevitable result of Gilbert's having served an important part of his playwriting apprenticeship with the German Reeds, whose "company had no villain."[49] But I would suggest that it had more fundamentally to do with his hard-won understanding of the bourgeois reluctance to confront the seamy side of human nature.

Of course, the high Savoy operas have characters whose actions impede progress toward the happy endings. Without such "blocking figures," conflict and plot would not exist. But, despite their unpleasant function, Gilbert allows few of them to be or remain entirely unsympathetic. In *Iolanthe,* for example, the characters who put obstacles on the paths of lovers are not the hypocrites that their equivalents in traditional comedy so frequently are: the Fairy Queen represses her own passion for Private Willis at the same time as she forbids her subjects to marry mortals, and the Lord Chancellor places legalistic restraints on his own suit to Phyllis no less than he does on Strephon's. If Sir Joseph orders Ralph off to a dungeon cell in the penultimate scene of *Pinafore,* he also seals the bond between the young lovers in the ultimate scene, benevolently joining their hands and admonishing the hero: "Here—take her, sir, and mind you treat her kindly" (97). And though the Pirate King may temporarily tear Frederic away from Mabel, even he and his fellow outlaws are not without their redeeming quality: "Because, with all our faults, we love our queen" (134).

The Pirate King voices this patriotic sentiment as he and his band surrender themselves to law. The surrender is automatic (and thus, in Bergsonian terms, funny): the Sergeant of Police has but to mention "Victoria's name" (134), and the pirates are immediately on their knees. And here we approach the essence of Gilbert's characterization: with a handful of significant exceptions, the inclination to submit the fate and desires of the self to the governance of law is programmed into his creatures from the start. Aristotle defines "ethos," the "ethical element . . . in the drama," to include "such things as reveal the moral bias of the agents—their tendency to choose or avoid a certain line of action, in cases where the motive is not obvious."[50] And law is clearly central to the benign ethos of the high Savoy characters.

Examples abound, even where we might least expect to find them. When the pirates, described by Frederic as "Men who stick at no offences," burst in to seize Mabel's sisters, the dramatic situation seems to portend rape—but the intent of these outlaws proves entirely legalistic, as they immediately announce their plan to be "conjugally matrimonified" to their captives (120). They are laughable, to be sure, but they are also honorable—just as they are in following their unprofitable policy of "never attacking a weaker party" than themselves (114). Again, though traditional comedy may lead us to expect young people zealously to assert their right to choose their own mates, Marco and Giuseppe waive theirs in *The Gondoliers,* agreeing instead to let their brides be chosen by the law of chance in a game of blindman's buff:

> A bias to disclose
> Would be indelicate—
(352)   And therefore we propose
> To let impartial Fate
> Select for us a mate!

It is a silly way to settle on a lifelong partner, but it is also appealingly chivalrous. More surprising still is the behavior of Luiz, a young man in the same opera who is confronted with the standard problem of the comic hero: he is forbidden by some higher authority to have the girl he loves. But rather than rebelling, as his more traditional brethren would, he readily accepts that his Casilda was legally bound in infancy to one of the two gondoliers, and even "obediently goes off to help settle which of the other two men will get the woman he loves."[51] Of course, the nursemaid he brings back reveals that Casilda's lawful husband is neither Marco nor Giuseppe but rather Luiz himself. He passively trusted in law, and law has delivered him:

LUIZ: When others claimed thy dainty hand,
I waited—waited—waited—waited.
DUKE: As prudence (so I understand)
Dictated—tated—tated—tated
(374–75)   CASILDA: By virtue of our early vow
Recorded—corded—corded—corded
DUCHESS: Your pure and patient love is now
Rewarded—warded—warded—warded.

These lines may be taken to express not only the moral of Luiz's story but also a central truth of the high Savoy operas. If, as the Mikado says, "virtue" is "triumphant . . . in theatrical performances" (265), then it is clear in these librettos that virtue is equated with submissiveness to law, for such is the distinguishing characteristic of Gilbert's victors.

Nowhere is this virtue more conspicuous than in his heroes, and no other Savoy characters more vividly testify to Gilbert's deviations from the established norms of characterization. As suggested above, the traditional comic hero is engaged "in relentless guerrilla warfare with society," inasmuch as society's "morality and accepted standards" usually stand between him and his happiness. Langer notes that the hero himself is usually responsible for realizing this happiness: "his fight is with obstacles and enemies, which his strength, wisdom, virtue, or other assets let him overcome." The quality least likely to be found among such a hero's panoply of virtues is obedience to externally imposed laws or codes: rather, "He is a hedonist who lives for the moment" without "any moral, ethical, or religious commitments."[52]

But he was not prominently featured at the Savoy. Some of Gilbert's heroes attempt to become the active and effective agents of their own happiness, but their attempts are invariably frustrated and sometimes even backfire. Ralph plans to elope with Josephine but is apprehended before he even gets her off the *Pinafore;* Frederic initiates a campaign to exterminate the pirates but is reclaimed by them before he can get it underway; and Hilarion, wishing to claim the bride he married in infancy, disguises himself as a woman to gain admission to Ida's monosexual domain, but is soon unmasked and condemned to death for his troubles. More far-reaching consequences attend upon the initiative taken by Paramount, who boldly determines to free himself and his nation from the domination of the wise men by registering "his Crown and Country under / The Joint Stock Company's Act of Sixty-Two" (*Utopia [Limited]*, 402); the results are positive at first, but he later finds himself confronted with the revolution of a dissatisfied populace. And Ludwig, likewise, experiences a boomerang effect when he proposes to Rudolph the scheme of fixing the statutory duel between them: when he assumes the Grand Duke's "place, / With all its obligations" (429), he unhappily finds that these obligations include engagements to three different women.[53]

Moreover, Gilbert eventually wrings from each of his heroes, whether previously active or sedentary, an acknowledgment of impotence. Adversity in love immediately drives Ralph and Nanki-Poo to the verge of suicide. Strephon, unjustly spurned by Phyllis, shows little more backbone: after a brief and unsuccessful attempt to assert his innocence, he ceases all efforts on his own behalf and consigns his defense to the Fairy Queen. Other concessions of romantic defeat come from Fairfax and Hilarion, each of whom uses the metaphor of bondage to describe his quiescent state. The former sings that, since his escape, he is free "In all but heart," having lost his romantic liberty by marrying a woman whom he does not yet know to be Elsie:

(*Yeomen of the Guard*, 331)

> Bound to an unknown bride
> For good and ill;
> Ah, is not one so tied
> A prisoner still?

And Hilarion, captured and bound by Ida's attendants, is more pained by the psychological fetters of his hopeless love for her:

(*Princess Ida*, 228)

> Whom thou hast chained must wear his chain,
> Thou canst not set him free.
> He wrestles with his bonds in vain
> Who lives by loving thee!

This wail of defeat culminates in total despair ("If kindly death will set me free / Why should I fear to die?"), and it is not surprising that, when the beaten hero makes his final entrance of the opera, he is "still bound" (233).

More interesting, though, are those confessions of helplessness made as certain plots approach their climaxes and decisive action would therefore be most expected of their heroes. Ralph, arrested on Sir Joseph's orders, extends his shackled hands to Josephine and sings:

> Farewell, my own,
> Light of my life, farewell!
> For crime unknown,
> I go to a dungeon cell.

(Pinafore, 96)

And he then disappears into captivity while the plot is set straight by Buttercup. Mabel begs Frederic to save her family from the pirates, but he can only reply, "I would if I could, but I am not able" (134), after which he stands still and entirely silent for the rest of the opera. Grosvenor responds similarly to Patience's shock over his newly commonplace appearance ("I can't help it," he protests, "I'm not a free agent" [165]) and is only rescued from despair by the heroine's realization that he now qualifies for her unselfish love. Strephon is no more effectual in the second act than he was in the first: just as he earlier relied upon the Fairy Queen for help, he now places his fate in the hands of his mother, asking her to obtain the Lord Chancellor's consent to his marriage with Phyllis. Paramount, confronted with the rebellion of the Utopian people, can only turn to Zara and say "My daughter, this is a very unpleasant state of things. What is to be done?" (411); though she shows herself a true heroine as she saves her country with her proposal for Government by Party, her father has clearly shown himself a less than masterful hero. And Ludwig falls apart when the Princess of Monte Carlo becomes the last in a long series of women to claim his hand in matrimony: "Here's another!—the fourth in four-and-twenty hours! Would anybody else like to marry me? You ma'am—or you—anybody!" (*Grand Duke*, 438).

In each of these instances, the hero essentially says, "I can do no more"—and that is precisely what he does, resigning himself to passivity while law prepares his deliverance. In this respect, he parallels the heroes of melodrama who, similarly, are delivered by Providence. He also resembles them in that he must demonstrate his worthiness to be delivered. Such worthiness consists not merely in a negative passivity but also in an affirmative obedience to law. Thus, Frederic follows whither his indentures lead him; the perfectly beautiful Grosvenor refuses to gain Patience's unselfish love by disguising or disfiguring himself, because "I am a trustee for Beauty, and it is my duty to see that the conditions of my trust are faithfully discharged" (153); Strephon will not elope with Phyllis without first seeking the consent of the Lord Chancellor; Nanki-Poo only runs off with Yum-Yum after he has been explicitly directed to do so by her legal guardian; and Ludwig, as an actor, submits his personal romantic preferences to the arbitration of the "dramatic contracts" (*Grand Duke,* 438) that dictate the relationships among him and all his troupe.

Gilbert's heroines are no less worthy. As the leading juvenile female's prime significance in each opera is usually romantic, the most striking demonstration she can make of her legalistic ethos is to bestow her heart or hand as law directs. So Patience does, loving first Bunthorne and then Grosvenor as the principle of unselfishness requires. Mabel offers to love Frederic and lead him back to the path of virtue because she feels "the moral beauty / Of making worldly interest / Subordinate to sense of duty" (118). Ida discovers her affection for Hilarion only when she is compelled to do so by Hildebrand's legalistic logic and by the law of Nature which requires her to mate ("Take him," Blanche tells her, "he is your Shall. Give in to Fate!" [234]). Julia less cheerfully agrees that, should Ernest's theatrical company succeed in their conspiracy to elevate him to the grand ducal throne, she will honor her contractual commitment to act as leading lady in all his productions: "My good sir, throughout my career I have made it a rule never to allow private feeling to interfere with my professional duties. You may be quite sure that (however distasteful the part may be), if I undertake it, I shall consider myself professionally bound to throw myself into it with all the ardour at my command." (427) Clearly,

Gilbert's, and our, perspective on some of these characters partakes of irony: if Mabel's sisters prompt us to wonder about the purity of her motives ("The question is, had he not been / A thing of beauty / Would she be swayed by quite as keen / A sense of duty?" [118]), we need no help to perceive the egotism of Grosvenor's duteousness or the drive toward self-aggrandizement that informs Julia's. But the characters themselves neither remark upon nor otherwise display awareness that such complications are present in their responses. Their apparent sincerity preserves their moral credit.

Of course, not every Savoy character is imbued with quite so much legalistic virtue, but even the exceptions to the prevalent benignity were well calculated to please Gilbert's patrons. For Gilbert himself was heir to the "fundamental melodramatic belief . . . that virtue is associated with lowliness and crime with rank, a supposition highly satisfying to the middle-class," and many among his targeted audience shared "the contempt for the 'unworking' aristocrat which the bourgeois invariably feels."[54] Even the later Victorian middle class, wishing though they did to blend in with the aristocracy, would have quietly continued to nurture a sense of moral superiority, knowing that they had not been undeservingly born to an exalted station but rather had earned their social dignity. At the same time, their recent successful struggle up the economic ladder had inevitably involved not only hypocrisy against their avowed ethical principles of self-denial but also cupidity—indeed, few Victorian social phenomena have been more eagerly commented upon than the gap between practice and profession in the lives of the ostensibly upright bourgeoisie. And the gnawing consciousness of these sins must significantly have diminished the pleasure of their self-congratulation. Thus, they can only have been delighted by the assurances offered by the Savoy operas that hypocrisy and greed were, after all, exclusively attributes of the aristocracy.

Nowhere is Gilbert's intention of associating hypocrisy with noble birth more evident than in *Patience*. The aesthetes who populate the piece are manifestly poseurs, affected in mannerism, speech, and dress. Bunthorne even admits his hypocrisy to the audience, confidentially confessing himself "an aesthetic sham"

(150), while the aesthetic maidens demonstrate theirs by loving the perfect Grosvenor, a blatant violation of Lady Angela's preachment to Patience about unselfish love. But only at a relatively late stage of the libretto's development did Gilbert determine to make these hypocrites aristocrats, and the deliberateness of his proceeding suggests that he was also determined to make a point. Previously, he had cast the two chief rivals of the piece as clergymen and laid the scene at the "country Vicarage" of the "Revd. Lawn Tennison." But, finding himself "crippled at every turn by the necessity of protecting myself from a charge of irreverence," he recast his clerics as poets. However, at the same time that he transformed Tennison into Bunthorne, he also moved the action to "Castle Bunthorne" (145), thus suggesting the poet's aristocratic status. Bunthorne's rival, Grosvenor, was now presented as "a man of propertee" (152); Angela, Ella, Saphir, and Sister Jane—the maidens who pine for Tennison's love—became Lady Angela, Lady Ella, Lady Saphir, and Lady Jane; and the line which had described the vicar's female admirers as "Young and pretty" came to read "Young and wealthy" (148) by the time that Jessie Bond sang it on stage.[55] Clearly, Gilbert was not concerned that audiences who might have been offended by hypocrites in clerical clothing would object to them in aristocratic guise. On the contrary, he must have known that his picture of the aesthete who neither sows nor reaps but merely gushes and mopes would correspond quite satisfactorily to the bourgeois conception of the aristocratic idler.

If the hypocrisy of these aesthetes caused Gilbert to turn them into aristocrats, we may find it interesting also to note that, when the Palmieri brothers in *The Gondoliers* learn that they are actually aristocrats, they immediately turn into hypocrites. A moment since, they were high-mindedly declaring their egalitarian political principles, but now that they have learned that one of them is a king, they begin backing and filling. "But which is it?" asks Marco:

(360)   DON ALHAMBRA: What does it matter? As you are both Republicans, and hold kings in abhorrence, of course you'll abdicate at once (going).

TESSA and GIANETTA: Oh, don't do that! (Marco and Giuseppe stop him.)
GIUSEPPE: Well, as to that, of course there are kings and kings. When I say I detest kings, I mean I detest *bad* kings.
DON ALHAMBRA: I see. It's a delicate distinction.

But perhaps the more striking evidence of Gilbert's intention to flatter the bourgeoisie at the aristocracy's expense is the high Savoy operas' displacement of the greed motive from the middle to the upper class. In pieces written before the crystallization of his comedic formula, avarice is common among characters of all social stations; thus, when Rowell remarks that "*Engaged* (1877) is undoubtedly Gilbert's most characteristic play" because "it exposes all its dramatis personae as motivated by money,"[56] he is surely correct insofar as the plays up to and including *Engaged* are concerned. Nor are the bourgeois characters of his early period especially exempt from this vice: examples of avarice among them include Ebenezer Tare (*Ages Ago*), an alderman and tallow chandler; the Smaileys (*Charity*), who are untitled country gentry; and Caroline (*Tom Cobb*), daughter of the shabby-genteel Effinghams. But in the more benignly populated high Savoy operas, the overall incidence of greed is markedly lower: we find, for instance, such mercenary women as Caroline Effingham, Adina (*Dulcamara*), Angelina (*Trial By Jury*), and Belinda, Minnie, and Maggie (*Engaged*) now replaced by such noble heroines as Josephine (*Pinafore*), Mabel (*The Pirates of Penzance*), Phyllis (*Iolanthe*), Yum-Yum (*The Mikado*), and Casilda (*The Gondoliers*), all of whom give their hearts to men whom they initially believe to be much poorer and humbler than themselves. And, inasmuch as greed occurs at all in Gilbert's mature librettos, it does so exclusively in his aristocratic characters. Pooh-Bah, for example, describes himself as "a particularly haughty and exclusive person, of pre-Adamite ancestral descent" but is nonetheless available for hire by nearly anyone: "I go and dine with middle-class people on reasonable terms. I dance at cheap suburban parties for a moderate fee. I accept refreshment at any hands, however lowly. I also retail state secrets at a very low figure" (*Mikado*, 247). He is, in short, a parasite, battening upon the middle class. In this he resembles the Duke and Duchess of Plaza-Toro, who come to make a substantial part of their living from getting "second-rate Aldermen knighted" and appearing at bourgeois social functions:

> DUCHESS: At middle-class party
>   I play at *écarté*—
>   And I'm by no means a beginner—
> DUKE (significantly): She's not a beginner.
> DUCHESS: To one of my station
>   The remuneration—
>   Five guineas a night and my dinner—
> DUKE: And wine with her dinner.

(*Gondoliers,* 371–72)

Pooh-Bah takes bribes, and the Duke and Duchess stand ready to "kindle / The spark of a swindle" (372). In the high Savoy operas, aristocratic greed merges with dishonesty.

But aristocrats who exercise local magisterial authority over their societies are a different matter altogether: their close association with law redeems them. In *Princess Ida,* for instance, King Hildebrand may be a bit of a bully, but he is neither a blocking character nor unsympathetic. Rather, he consistently exerts his authority to promote the union of hero and heroine, and he is venerated by his subjects: "My Lord, we love our king. / His wise remarks are valued by his court / As precious stones" (216). (King Gama, on the other hand, exercises no present power over any portion of the world that we actually see in the play, and he is not so favorably presented.) Paramount is just as popular as Hildebrand, as even the malign wise men admit:

> Of a tyrant polite
> He's a paragon quite.
> He's as modest and mild
> In his ways as a child;
> And no one ever met
> With an autocrat, yet,
> So delightfully bland
> To the least in the land!

(*Utopia [Limited],* 387)

Even the Mikado, tinged though he is with sadism, appears to be a well-liked and well-intentioned ruler. Pish-Tush calls him "Our great Mikado, virtuous man" (246), while the monarch himself boasts of his "very humane endeavour" to mete out punishments that will provide his subjects not only justice but also "innocent merriment" (262).

Along with his passive heroes, Gilbert's benign authority figures represent his most radical and significant departure from traditional characterization. For, as Frye suggests, it had not been the standard practice of comedy to accord much respect to the powers ruling over either the microcosm of the family or the macrocosm of society:

> *The obstacles to the hero's desire, then, form the action of comedy, and the overcoming of them the comic resolution. The obstacles are usually parental, hence comedy often turns on a clash between a son's and a father's will. Thus the comic dramatist as a rule writes for the younger men in his audience, and the older members of almost any society are apt to feel that comedy has something subversive about it. . . . The opponent of the hero's wishes, when not the father, is generally someone who partakes of the father's closer relation to established society: that is, a rival with less youth and more money. . . . The fury with which these characters are baited and exploded from the stage shows that they are father-surrogates, and even if they were not, they would still be usurpers and their claim to possess the girl must be shown up as somehow fraudulent. They are, in short, impostors, and the extent to which they have real power implies some criticism of the society that allows them their power.*[57]

Conversely, affirmation of a society requires sympathetic characterization of magisterial figures of all sorts—kings and judges, fathers and guardians. Such affirmation was central to Gilbert's agenda; thus, if selfishness and imposture distinguish those who wield law's authority in traditional comedy, fairness and honesty mark their counterparts in the high Savoy operas.

Fairness consists in abiding by the laws one serves and enforces. Those few magistrates who act without this virtue give

Gilbert the opportunity to show how important he thought it. None of them prospers. Grand Duke Rudolph, for instance, extorts money from his subjects by mandating the purchase of goods on which he holds monopolies or for which he receives kickbacks; he also conspires with Ludwig to fix their statutory duel and so to subvert the law by which his own realm provides for the resolution of disputes. As a direct result of the latter act, he is consigned to what very nearly becomes a permanent legal death. Similarly, Ko-Ko and Pooh-Bah, magistrates of Titipu who are readily willing to bribe and be bribed in making the law serve their own ends, bring themselves to the verge of actual death as a direct result of their efforts to subvert the Mikado's arbitrary but lawful demand for an execution. Scaphio and Phantis, who have long used their public offices to enrich themselves, may actually have to cross this verge in *Utopia (Limited):* we last see them "led off in custody" with Paramount declaring, "Your hour has come already—away with them, and let them wait my will" (412). Less serious, but no less clear, are the consequences that attend upon Sir Joseph's selfish use of his legal powers in *Pinafore*. Piqued by Josephine's preference for another man, he first threatens to court-martial her father and then, "for crime unknown" (96), sends her lover to prison. But this final injustice backfires, as it moves Buttercup finally to make the revelation that, ironically, puts the Captain's daughter beyond Sir Joseph's matrimonial horizons.

In contrast to Sir Joseph stands the Lord Chancellor. No other high Savoy character more completely identifies himself with law:

> The Law is the true embodiment
> Of everything that's excellent.
> It has no kind of fault or flaw,
> And I, my lords, embody the law.

(*Iolanthe,* 183–84)

And no other high Savoy magistrate more fully and fairly enforces the restraints of law upon his own will—even when it causes him considerable pain to do so. As Phyllis's legal guardian, he refuses to favor his own desire to become Phyllis's husband, even though "My regard for her is rapidly undermining my constitution. Three months ago I was a stout man. . . . If I could reconcile it with my duty, I should unhesitatingly award her to myself, for I can conscientiously say that I know no man who is so well-fitted to render her exceptionally happy. But such an award would be open to misconstruction, and therefore, at whatever personal inconvenience, I waive my claim" (184). We should not be surprised that the Peers whom he presides over regard him as "a very just and kindly old gentleman" (198).

Honesty consists in truthfulness, to oneself as well as others. In the *Philebus,* Plato discusses the role of self-deceit in comedy, maintaining that "the nature of the ridiculous" consists in not knowing oneself; that is, a man is ridiculous if he fancies himself richer or taller or morally better than he actually is. However, "All who are silly enough to entertain this lying conceit of themselves may, of course, be divided like the rest of mankind into two classes—one having power and might, and the other the reverse. . . . Those of them who are weak and unable to revenge themselves, when they are laughed at, may be truly called ridiculous. . . . Ignorance in the powerful is hateful and horrible, because hurtful to others both in reality and in fiction."[58] Those who identified their interests with the maintenance of the established order, as Gilbert's bourgeois audiences did, would find nothing funny about self-deceiving magistrates.

Consequently, Gilbert took special care to assure these audiences that his civic magistrates—and, by implication, theirs—were not lacking in self-knowledge. His chief means of doing so became the autobiographical songs which play so prominent a part in the fame of the Savoy operas. Goldberg calls them "those seemingly innocent ditties which fairly disrobe the character before his listening public and parade him in his nakedness," for the singers "are under some compulsion to speak the inner truth."[59] But the compulsion is never external; rather, each magisterial autobiographer makes a fully voluntary confession of the flaws in his temperament, gaps in his knowledge, and deficiencies of his professional background. Examples range from the first to the last of the high Savoy operas:

Sir Joseph sings two such songs when he first boards the *Pinafore.* "I am the monarch of the sea" (85) reveals the First Lord of the Admiralty's distaste for actually going out to sea, while "When I was a lad" (85–86) cheerfully confesses that his promotion to "Ruler of the Queen's Navee" had nothing whatsoever to do with intellectual acuteness or knowledge of matters nautical.[60]

When the Sergeant of Police and his men, the law's chief representatives in *The Pirates of Penzance,* first appear in that opera, they immediately admit their fears about their upcoming battle with the pirates. As self-confessed "Calculated men . . . / Who are going to meet their fate . . . / In a highly nervous state" (126), they are antitheses of the *miles gloriosus* (or braggart soldier), one of traditional comedy's most common species of impostor.

When the Lord Chancellor sings "When I went to the Bar as a very young man" (*Iolanthe,* 186–87), he frankly reveals that "my advancement to my present distinguished position" owed much more to conscientiousness and circumspection than to legal knowledge or skill.

Ko-Ko tells us just a little of his background in the solo "Taken from the county jail" (*Mikado,* 248) which interrupts the chorus sung in honor of his first entrance; it is, however, enough to make plain that his professional rise was not based upon mastery of the functions of a Lord High Executioner.

When Ludwig, having become chief magistrate of Pfennig Halbpfennig, dresses himself in classical Greek attire and announces his plan to run his court along ancient Athenian lines, he has dropped only a few learned references and foreign phrases before he feels it necessary to confide:

> At this juncture I may mention
> That this erudition sham
> Is but classical pretension,
> The result of steady "cram":
> Periphrastic methods spurning,
> To this audience discerning
> I admit this show of learning
> Is the fruit of steady "cram!"

(*Grand Duke,* 440)

And the chorus echoes him, for the autobiographical confessions of all Gilbert's high Savoy magistrates are meant to be fully public acts. Only Bunthorne—an aristocratic poseur with no magisterial authority—waits until he is fully alone to sing the truth about himself.

Irony, to be sure, is at work in these songs, and its humor would not have been lost on the newly risen bourgeoisie in Gilbert's audience, who would immediately have recognized—as the autobiographers apparently do not—that in seeking professional advancement, it is wiser not to trumpet one's own incompetence. At the same time, though, the frankness with which these characters reveal themselves prevents their being exposed as impostors, and the disarming amiability of their revelations protects them from being "baited and exploded from the stage." Indeed, while the new society of comedy normally coalesces around and focuses on the triumphant hero, the assembled joyful choruses in the finales of *Pinafore* and *Iolanthe* fix their attention elsewhere. They sing their final words in praise of their plays' chief magistrates, an honor that Gilbert accords none of his heroes.

Parental authorities are presented no less respectfully. Fathers are the prime impostors of traditional comedy; as previously noted, the *senex iratus* is among the most common type of *alazon,* and the action of many a comedy turns upon the claim made by a father or father surrogate "to possess the girl"—a claim which "must be shown up as somehow fraudulent." But Gilbert allows few of his father figures to make such a claim, thus shielding them from the exposure and humiliation attendant thereupon. And in three of the four instances in which an older man does romantically compete with a younger, the former is never truly defeated. Rather, Sir Joseph voluntarily withdraws as a candidate for Josephine's hand when the revelation of her father's identity demotes her to the very lowest social class (love may level all ranks, he admits, "to a considerable extent, but it does not level them as much as that" [*Pinafore,* 97]); the Lord Chancellor loses all interest in Phyllis when he learns that his beloved Iolanthe is still alive; and Scaphio and Phantis, after their initial burst of erotic enthusiasm for Zara, apparently forget not only the princess but also their young rival Fitzbattleaxe. Only Ko-Ko is truly forced to yield up the girl he loves to a younger man.

More remarkably, the tendency of Savoy fathers is either to object benevolently to their children's romantic choices or not to object at all. Captain Corcoran clearly disapproves of Ralph as a suitor for Josephine's hand and prefers that she accept Sir Joseph, but he gains our esteem when he tenderly declares that "In a matter of the heart I would not coerce my daughter" (*Pinafore,* 84). He certainly retains Josephine's affection—as the Lord Chancellor does Phyllis's, despite his expressed objections to Strephon. In other cases where parental opposition might be expected, Gilbert simply avoids the situation by keeping the fathers in ignorance. The Duke of Plaza-Toro is unaware of Casilda's love for his servant Luiz until Luiz ascends the throne of Barataria and so becomes a worthy husband for her, while King Paramount is never told of his daughter's attachment to Captain Fitzbattleaxe, whose social status might make him objectionable as her suitor. And in still other cases, fathers indicate approval of their children's desires: the Major-General has, by the second act, tacitly accepted the ex-pirate Frederic as a prospective son-in-law, while Hildebrand aggressively promotes his son's love for Ida from the first.

But the benignity that normally distinguishes Gilbert's authority figures, heroes, and heroines is hardly to be found in *Ruddigore,* an odd and ill-advised reversion toward traditional characterization. To begin with, the lords of the manor in the village of Rederring have all, *ipso facto,* been criminals, for all the baronets of Ruddigore have been victims of the witch's curse requiring the commission of a daily crime—indeed, this curse is explained as having been the direct result of the first baronet's ruthless abuse of his local judicial powers. And though the present rightful baronet sings the inevitable autobiographical song, it only serves to intensify our uneasiness about him. For we hear Robin claim that he is "diffident, modest, and shy" (284) at the same time as he unblushingly describes his unrivaled wit, distinctively intellectual appearance, and unparalleled range of artistic talents: clearly he must be lying about either his humility or his other assets. That he is not actually in possession of his magisterial office at the time he sings this song only partially qualifies our response to it.

And if Robin lacks the frank honesty of most high Savoy

authority figures, he likewise lacks the passive, legalistic ethos of most high Savoy heroes. Indeed, he has spent the last twenty years before the rise of the curtain avoiding his obligation to assume his legal title and the curse that goes with it; later, when he is installed as Sir Ruthven, the ghosts come to tell him that the "crimes" he has committed fulfill neither the letter nor the spirit of this curse. He ultimately becomes the only hero in the entire series who not only attempts to become the active and effective agent of his own happiness but actually succeeds in doing so. For it is Robin's syllogistic ingenuity that nullifies the effects of the witch's curse, shifts the problematic baronetcy back to the shoulders of one of his resurrected ancestors, and qualifies him once again as the preferred object of Rose's love. He is, in short, a throwback to the traditional comic hero.

Nor are the other two characters in *Ruddigore*'s love triangle cut from Gilbert's usual cloth. Dick Dauntless professes submissive obedience to his conscience, but the morality of the actions it dictates to him is highly suspect. When he first goes to court Rose on Robin's behalf and sees how pretty she is, conscience immediately authorizes him to betray his trust: "The moment I see her, and just as I was a-goin' to mention your name, my heart it up and it says, says it—'Dick, you've fell in love with her yourself,' it says; 'Be honest and sailor-like—don't skulk under false colours—speak up' it says, 'take her, you dog, and with her my blessin'!'" (286) And, when Robin subsequently gets the better of him in their romantic competition, Dick suddenly feels himself compelled to break Robin's confidence by revealing that his rival is the officially wicked baronet of Ruddigore: "That's what my heart says. It says 'Dick,' it says . . . 'That there young gal would recoil from him if she knowed what he really were. Ought you to stand off and on, and let this young gal take this false step and never fire a shot across her bows to bring her to? No,' it says, 'you did *not* ought.' And I won't ought, accordin'." (290) The self-serving hypocrisy of all this is clear enough.

The object of these men's affections is their moral and spiritual peer. While other Savoy heroines are conspicuous for their lack of avarice, Rose Maybud's affinities are with those more mercenary young women whom Gilbert featured in his pre-*Pinafore* plays. When she expresses her preference for Robin over Dick, she makes clear that she has taken a detailed inventory of the possessions of each: "Oh, but sir, I knew not that thou didst seek me in wedlock, or in very truth I should not have hearkened unto this man, for behold, he is but a lowly mariner, and very poor withal, whereas thou art a tiller of land, and thou hast fat oxen, and many sheep and swine, a considerable dairy farm, and much corn and oil!" (286) Not surprisingly, she soon afterward abandons Dick in favor of Robin—only one of five instances in which she transfers her romantic preference to a more advantageous mate. Like Dick, she pretends to a legalistic ethos, using her book of etiquette as he does his conscience. But, as Earl F. Bargainnier says, she quotes it "as the devil quotes scripture. Rose is able to justify any desire or action on her part by referring to it."[61]

Unlike any other work in the high Savoy series, *Ruddigore* was hissed at its premiere by what the *Times* called "a small but very determined minority" of the audience. Twenty years later, Gilbert was still defending himself and his partner from the charge that the opera represented a blemish on their record of success: "We are credited—or discredited—with one conspicuous failure, *Ruddigore; or, The Witch's Curse*. Well, it ran eight months, and, with the sale of the libretto, put £7,000 into my pocket."[62] His point is not invalid; *Ruddigore* did, after all, run longer than three of the other ten high Savoy operas. But the piece's success was not such as he and Sullivan had, by 1887, come to expect: it achieved, for instance, fewer than half the performances encompassed by the first run of *The Mikado,* its immediate predecessor.

If *Ruddigore* stands as an anomaly in the record of the partnership's fortunes at the box office, the explanation may be found in the anomalous approach that its librettist took to characterization. "It is this combination of selfish leading characters," says Stedman, "completely devoid of qualities with which the audience may make that identification which even artificial comedy requires to some degree, which must account for the basic initial reaction to *Ruddygore*." Sullivan shared this view: when Gilbert first presented him a scenario for the piece, the disappointed composer wrote in his diary that "it is a 'puppet-show' and not human. It is impossible to feel sympathy with a single person."[63] Gilbert's bourgeois patrons, loyal though they had become by the time of the piece's premiere, could only be pushed so far, and the rogues' gallery that he spread before them in *Ruddigore* must have been a gross affront to their sentimental sensibilities.

Law and Love

Law in the high Savoy operas does not stand in the same relationship to love as it does to plot and character. While law informs and vitalizes Gilbert's action and his people—initiating and resolving the former, motivating and molding the latter—it serves rather to displace love, usurping the traditional place of juvenile romance as the thematic focus of comedy.

As we have seen, Gilbert's plots develop syllogistically. The major premise typically embodies a problematic law which creates a conflict for the sympathetic characters between duty and desire, though the desire in question is not necessarily erotic. Inasmuch as plot represents the working out of conflict, the climax of each opera is that event (either the discovery of the minor premise or the reinterpretation of the major premise) which enables these characters to reconcile duty with desire, while the denouement toward which the action drives is the actual resolution of the problem initially posed by law. The problem of who will marry the heroine is distinctly subordinate in importance.

To be sure, the solutions to both problems are sometimes identical, for the central laws of certain operas bear directly on their heroines' matrimonial options and obligations. *Pinafore*'s major premise is "captains' daughters don't marry foremast jacks" (83); the problem disappears when Ralph is discovered to be no foremast jack and Josephine no captain's daughter. The rule about unselfishness in love that governs the world of *Patience* forbade the title character to love the perfectly beautiful Grosvenor but authorizes her to accept him in his post-aesthetic incarnation. The legal problem of both *Princess Ida* and *The Gondoliers* is that the heroine of each is bound to a man she married in infancy; the operas are resolved when Ida learns to love the man she wed and Casilda learns that the man she wed is the man she loves. The solution to each of these love problems is directly related to the fulfillment of the law; the love plots of these pieces are therefore, formally, the main plots.

But in six of the eleven high Savoy operas, the heroine's love story is formally reduced to the status of subplot. The problematic major premise in each of these works—as expressed in the principle in *Pirates* that duty must be done, the fairy law of *Iolanthe,* the Mikado's demand for an execution, the witch's curse in *Ruddigore,* the royal decree for the Anglicization of Utopia, and the code of the duello in *The Grand Duke*—has little enough to do with the heroine and no direct relationship to her present or future marital status. As in the other operas, the main plots aim primarily at satisfying the law; the result, in these six pieces, is that the resolution of the juvenile female's romantic problem becomes merely a by-product of the dramatic action.

Moreover, in all but two of the high Savoy operas, no matter what the formal status of the young lovers' story in the plot, Gilbert uses a variety of devices to diminish their prominence and deny the thematic significance that traditional comedy would attach to their union. One of the exceptions to this practice is *The Yeomen of the Guard,* which develops no syllogism and, as we have seen, aims at the fulfillment of love rather than law. The other is *Princess Ida,* which was even less successful than *Ruddigore,* and which I will presently propose as another instance in which Gilbert had to pay a price for deviating from his established dramaturgical norms.

The high Savoy approach to juvenile love was itself a deviation—both from the European tradition embodied in 2,000 years of New Comedy, and from the native tradition that Shakespeare had established almost 300 years before Gilbert's career began. "Nearly every English comedy," says Thorndike, "tells the story of a courtship resulting happily. The madcap girl sobers down, the scapegrace youth is tamed, the errant husband or wife returns, the sweet young innocents assume the responsibilities of the married state." Such marriages are thematically central in comedy because they betoken the perpetuation of the species, the triumph of human life over death. Shakespeare himself underlined this point with such speeches as Benedick's "I have railed so long against marriage. . . . No, the world must be peopled" in *Much Ado about Nothing* (2.3.217–21) and Hymen's "Wedding is great Juno's crown. . . . / 'Tis Hymen peoples every town" in *As You Like It* (5.4.135–37). Robert Corrigan summarizes:

> *That all comedy celebrates life's capacity to renew itself is underscored by the central presence of lovers in every comic action. There are invariably obstacles or misunderstandings for them to overcome—parents who separate them, mistaken identities, petty jealousies or temporary rivals, enforced absences, money problems—but by the end of the play, they are happily united, and the closing note is always bright with hope for the future. The lovers embody the energy and elation of that life, which is always pushing on.*[64]

Nevertheless, as Henry Ten Eyck Perry has observed, "there is an indication throughout Gilbert's work that he did not consider the relation between the sexes as a vital matter."[65] This attitude manifests itself in the behavior of his characters: as Phyllis Karr notes, "the principal Dragoon officers and Rapturous Ladies, Marco and Giuseppe and (at least in the beginning) Gianetta and Tessa, all show a carefree mix-and-match attitude to the whole business of love and mating."[66] Similarly offhand are Sir Joseph and Dick Dauntless, who respectively accept and claim the hands of Hebe and Zorah with no previous courtship or forethought; even less reflective are the pirates, who are ready to marry the Major-General's daughters the moment they see them. Such casually contrived unions hardly seem to be matters of great moment.

But Gilbert's expressed attitude toward love sometimes goes beyond mere indifference into outright cynicism. To be sure, he never allowed himself in the high Savoy operas to indulge in the thoroughgoing anti-sentimentalism of *Engaged,* in which every tender word spoken is merely a transparent cloak thrown over avarice or lust, but isolated love scenes in the librettos have an unmistakably sardonic ring. Thus, when Phyllis and Strephon are reconciled in the second act of *Iolanthe* and agree that they should wed immediately, they exchange the following fatalistic lines:

(199)

PHYLLIS: We won't wait long.
STREPHON: No—we might change our minds. We'll get married first.
PHYLLIS: And change our minds afterwards?
STREPHON: That's the usual course.

The Yeomen of the Guard likewise invites us to view love and marriage as divisible, especially when Phoebe explains how Wilfred has learned of the Merylls' role in Fairfax's escape and used his knowledge to blackmail her into betrothal:

(337)

PHOEBE: Oh, father, he discovered our secret through my folly, and the price of his silence is—
WILFRED: Phoebe's heart.
PHOEBE: Oh, dear no—Phoebe's hand.
WILFRED: It's the same thing!
PHOEBE: *Is* it!

Shortly afterward, when Dame Carruthers similarly traps Sergeant Meryll into wedlock, the same lines are repeated between them. And the last opera in the series, *The Grand Duke,* sounds its sour note only moments after the rise of the curtain, as the Dummkopf theatrical company, preparing for the nuptials of Ludwig and Lisa, hails their arrival in the following chorus:

(423)

Here they come, the couple plighted—
    On life's journey gaily start them.
Soon to be for aye united,
    Till divorce or death shall part them.

More interesting still are the duet and chorus which ring down the curtain of *The Mikado.* The juvenile lovers sing:

(268)

The threatened cloud has passed away,
And brightly shines the dawning day;
What though the night may come too soon,
We've years and years of afternoon!

The assembled company rejoices with them. As Sutton observes, the opera thus "allows the young to have their way. . . . With the emblems of Age, Repression, and Death now placated, the revelers can resume the chorus from the Act I finale. They celebrate dawn and life, while acknowledging . . . the night that comes too soon."[67] But the acknowledgment is jarring. If comedy celebrates "life's capacity to renew itself" through young lovers who "embody the energy and elation of that life, which is always pushing on," nothing could be more disharmonious with the hopeful spirit of such a celebration than an assertion of death's inevitability. But Gilbert seems frequently to have associated mortality with marriage: Arthur B. Brenner notes that marriage is a crime punishable by death for certain characters in *The Pretty Druidess* and *Iolanthe;* it entails death as its price for Nanki-Poo in *The Mikado* and for the corporal who seeks the hand of the Vivandiere in the Bab ballad entitled "The Two Majors"; and it is referred to as "our first death" in Gilbert's early comedy *An Old Score.*[68] I think we can say that Gilbert lacked confidence that sexual union represented the triumph of life.

His audiences can have been little more sanguine on this point. Nineteenth-century science had made it impossible for educated Victorians to believe that "life's capacity to renew itself" was unlimited in any species, including humanity. As the evidence on this point mounted, affirmations to the contrary must have seemed increasingly unconvincing—even when they were the merely implicit and fully conventional affirmations of comedy, and even when they were processed by the audience (as so much archetypal material is) in something less than full consciousness of their significance. Indeed, comedy's traditional story of the young and vital hero's victory over a less capable and virile rival for the heroine's hand may have started to become vaguely depressing, paralleling as it did the gloomy Darwinian account of survival of the fittest. For Darwin himself, comedic tales were an agreeable spur to escapism: in his *Autobiography,* written mostly in the seventies, the old scientist declared that he had lost interest in most literature; however, "novels, which are works of imagination, though not of a very high order, have been for years a wonderful relief and pleasure to me, and I often bless all novelists. A surprising number have been read aloud to me, and I like all, if moderately good, and if they do not end unhappily—against which a law ought to be passed." His particular preference was for stories that centered on "a pretty woman"[69]—whose happy ending, presumably, would be the comedically traditional one of marriage. But most Victorians were not as easily reconciled to Darwinism as Darwin and were unlikely to have been successful in duplicating the scientist's blithe detachment from the philosophical implications of such literature. In this climate, Gilbert may well have sensed that the apotheosis of young love would not necessarily be regarded by his patrons as the most joyful of comedic conclusions.

Consequently, his mature comedy denied young love the significance that traditional comedy assigned it. This accounts for the conspicuous absence in his high Savoy librettos of virtually all reference to the connection between marriage and procreation. Indeed, only two references to prospective parenthood exist in the entire series, and neither teems with hope for the future. In *Pinafore*, Josephine imagines herself living with Ralph in:

(93)

> a dark, dingy room
> In some back street, with stuffy children crying,
> Where organs yell, and clacking housewives fume,
> And clothes are hanging out all day a-drying.
> With one cracked looking-glass to see your face in,
> And dinner served up in a pudding basin!

And in *The Grand Duke*, as Julia sings of the "mock affection" she would bestow on Ernest were she to play the real-life part of his bride, she imagines a related role for herself:

(427)

> And should there come to me,
>   Some summers hence,
> In all the childish glee
>   Of innocence,
>   Fair babes, aglow with beauty vernal,
>   My heart would bound with joy diurnal!
>   This sweet display of sympathy maternal,
> Well, that would also be
>   A mere pretence!

Similar in spirit is *His Excellency,* a libretto written to music by
Osmond Carr just two years earlier. When Nanna contemplates
marriage with Erling, she finds herself incapable of uttering the
dreaded word "family":

> And then—who knows?—
>   Perhaps some day a fam—
>   Perhaps a famine!
> My argument's correct, if you examine,
> What should we do, if there should come a f-famine![70]

Gilbert himself rather liked children, and did not expect his audiences to bring to the theater a jaundiced perspective on parenthood. He was simply attempting to provide them a brief escape
from the Darwinian debate that hounded them down the nights and
down the days. To be sure, the librettos do not altogether avoid
references to so highly topical a subject as evolution: we find one in
Lady Psyche's attempt to demonstrate the superiority of Woman by
contrasting her with "Man" who, "sprung from an Ape, is Ape at
heart" (*Princess Ida,* 224), and we find another in Pooh-Bah's claim
to "pre-Adamite ancestral descent" from "a protoplasmal primor-
dial atomic globule" (*Mikado,* 247). But by keeping young love out
of the spotlight and dissociating it from the perpetuation of the
species, Gilbert simply avoided calling the question that his patrons
may have come to the Savoy to forget: in no sense did they have to
feel that their decision to applaud at the fall of the curtain had
anything to do with their faith, or lack of faith, in the future of
humanity.

But while Gilbert may have been the first important comic
dramatist to shape his approach to love in response to the anxieties
of the post-Darwinian age, he was not quite the first to minimize its
thematic importance. Among English authors, Ben Jonson stands
out as one, and almost the only, possible source of inspiration for his
practices—but I believe that Gilbert found his primary model in the
Old Comedy of Aristophanes. Aristophanes, of course, had had his
own reasons for de-emphasizing romantic love. He lived and wrote
near the end of the golden age of Athenian democracy and imperial-
ism and, like his audiences, had affairs of state foremost on his

mind. Women were excluded from participation in such affairs and, perhaps as a result, "the Athenians could make little intellectual or emotional contact with their wives"; thus, a "common absence of affection [persisted] between husband and wife . . . in Periclean Athens."[71] Therefore, we should not be surprised that the chief comic dramatist of the fifth century B.C. should have paid little attention to the genesis of such relatively uninteresting relationships. In the following century, as Athens's political importance declined, the fascinations of public affairs did so as well; thus, the New Comedy which appeared shortly after Aristophanes's death came to focus on domestic life and the marital relation upon which domestic life is founded. This focus persisted in the comedy that the Romans borrowed from the Greeks, that Shakespeare learned from Roman models, and that later English dramatists imitated from Shakespeare. To be sure, other dramatists besides Jonson explored alternative paths; indeed, in 1846, Planché made a valiant attempt to steer English comedy back toward Aristophanic principles by mounting an adaptation of *The Birds* at the Haymarket. But it found little favor with the public: as Rowell observes, "Neither his powers nor his period were apt for the purpose" of achieving "a change in theatrical taste to which W. S. Gilbert subsequently devoted the greater part of his life-work."[72]

Still, given the sentimentality prevalent among his bourgeois patrons, Gilbert could hardly have hoped to alter their taste so far as to make them accept comedy entirely lacking in romantic content. This he had recognized in the Prologue of *The Wicked World* (1873), which first informs the audience of the Author's intention to show "That love is not a blessing, but a curse!" but then reassures them:

> But pray do not suppose it's his intent
> To do without this vital element—
> His drama *would* be in a pretty mess!
> With quite as fair a prospect of success,
> Might a dispensing chemist in his den
> Endeavour to dispense with oxygen.[73]

Aristophanes can have furnished Gilbert few specific hints about how to subsume "this vital element" into his comedy, for the Greek master did what Gilbert dared not: his normal mode of treating the relation between the sexes was to ignore the subject entirely. There were, however, exceptions—the most notable being *Lysistrata*. Though the main characters of this play are already married, there is nonetheless an obstacle to the sexual union of man and woman, just as there inevitably is in those later "New" comedies which are concerned with premarital romantic problems. But, while the standard plot of post-Aristophanic comedy makes removal of this obstacle the means to the end of sexual union, *Lysistrata* reverses cause and effect. The barrier between the sexes is the war between Athens and Sparta, and the true denouement toward which Aristophanes drives his action is the establishment of peace. When the wives finally bargain to resume sexual relations with their husbands, they do so only as a means of achieving this political end; erotic union—or, in this case, reunion—thus becomes merely the cause of the happy ending, not the happy ending itself. For the frustrated men, of course, the causality is reversed—that is, the making of peace is their means of regaining their conjugal rights— but Aristophanes consistently develops his action from the women's perspective, beginning with their resolve to withhold their bodies from their husbands and ending with a celebration of the peace they have sought. Even the men enter into the spirit of this celebration, as they apparently forget their sexual urgencies and, instead of rushing home with their wives, conclude the play by singing and dancing in honor of their treaty and of the virgin goddesses Artemis and Athena. The emphasis of this final scene makes clear that the erotic action of *Lysistrata* is subordinate in importance to its political action.

Indeed, for Aristophanes, the former probably became thematically significant only when placed in the context of the latter. And Gilbert's search for a comedic model may have drawn him to Greek Old Comedy because he sensed that its priorities were such that his audiences would find congenial. Like Aristophanes and his contemporaries, the Victorian bourgeoisie accorded greater importance to that which affected the common welfare than to that which merely concerned the individual will. As Sutton says of Gilbert's librettos, "Because the chorus has such prominence, the action

tends to affect the complete society depicted on stage. . . . The plot
is almost never limited to the problems of the main characters: their
difficulties are part of some larger predicament, especially in the last
three operas where the emphasis becomes more political than personal, and the theme expresses a concern of Aristophanes—the
governing of a state."[74] The consistency with which Gilbert resolved nearly all his high Savoy love problems within the larger
context of law suggests that his perspective and practices were
"Aristophanic" throughout the prime of his career.

Just as Aristophanes puts aside the issue of sexual love before
the final scene of *Lysistrata,* Gilbert frequently leaves behind his
juvenile love plots before the finales of his Savoy operas. As Thorndike's comments suggest, such a practice is wholly out of keeping
with comedic tradition; instead, "Nearly every comedy . . . assumes that the love of A for B or B for A is the most important thing
in the universe. . . . The man is pursuing the woman, or the woman
is pursuing the man, and the interest in life is supposed to be
exhausted by the capture, or the escape."[75] But in *Iolanthe,* the
action continues even after Phyllis and Strephon have reached their
final decision to marry. They fade into the background soon after
doing so, and the interest is then concentrated on uniting the fairies
with the peers, the Fairy Queen with Private Willis, and, most importantly, on reuniting the Lord Chancellor with Iolanthe, whose
status as title character suggests her centrality to the piece. Likewise, in *The Mikado,* the marital vows of Nanki-Poo and Yum-
Yum are signed, sealed, and delivered early in the second act; while
the lovers then wait (mostly offstage) for the finale, the play's
attention turns to Ko-Ko's dealings with the monarch and his
courtship of Katisha. And, in *Utopia (Limited),* the juvenile love
story simply drops out of the plot, which never resolves or even
returns to the romantic problem created for Zara and Fitzbattleaxe
by the preemptive courtship paid her in the first act by the two wise
men. The evidence suggests that this lack of closure was fully
considered: before *Utopia* premiered, Gilbert wrote but chose to
discard two alternative scenes in which Fitzbattleaxe dissuades
Scaphio and Phantis from their marital aspirations.[76]

By the time he wrote *Utopia (Limited),* "Gilbert had already
done more, perhaps, than most dramatists to wean his audience

away from obsession with young love," claims Karr—adding that, in *Utopia* itself, King Paramount and Lady Sophy provide "the primary love interest."[77] The relationship of these older lovers continues to occupy both the stage and our sympathies well after the ardor of Zara and Fitzbattleaxe has been effectively forgotten. Thus, Gilbert not only neglects his heroine's love story but pushes her out of the spotlight, replacing her with a mature bride-to-be whose forthcoming marriage is unlikely to have any bearing on the perpetuation of the species. Other operas make the same substitution. The romantic fates of Iolanthe (who may appear youthful but is, in fact, "a couple of centuries or so" in age [199]) and Katisha (who is evidently free to choose her own husband and must therefore be beyond the "years of indiscretion" which, in Gilbert's Japan, are "from seventeen to forty-nine" [*Mikado*, 251]) remain at the center of our attention after Phyllis and Yum-Yum have been consigned to their future husbands. Again, in the final scene of *Patience*, Gilbert first has the young heroine rush to Grosvenor's arms and then sets the couple aside as the Duke steps forward to declare his decision to bestow his name and rank upon the silver-haired Lady Jane, who thus upstages the title character as the curtain falls. Still other finales feature post-maternal women who may not altogether supplant the heroines but whose prospective nuptials are given just as much prominence. They include Buttercup in *Pinafore*, who is old enough to have been her future husband's nursemaid; the Fairy Queen, who is at least as old as Iolanthe and often played as older; and Dame Hannah in *Ruddigore*, whose age is never specified but who is described by Zorah as "a nice old person" (279).

In *Princess Ida*, however, youthful passion is the exclusive order of the day, and no juvenile character is immune to it. Ida herself resists but ultimately succumbs to Nature's demand that she mate and procreate; the hitherto cloistered Melissa, on the other hand, immediately melts at the sight of Florian:

> MELISSA: Is this indeed a man?
> I've often heard of them, but, till to-day,
> (224–25)   Never set eyes on one. They told me men
> Were hideous, idiotic, and deformed!
> They're quite as beautiful as women are!

As beautiful—they're infinitely more so!
Their cheeks have not that pulpy softness which
One gets so weary of in womankind:
Their features are more marked—and—oh their chins!
How curious! (Feeling his chin.)
FLORIAN: I fear it's rather rough.
MELISSA: (eagerly) Oh don't apologize—I like it so!

Especially striking is the argument she uses to justify the rightness of her newly stirred feelings:

(225)

My natural instinct teaches me
    (And instinct is important, O!)
You're everything you ought to be,
    And nothing that you oughtn't, O!

This is only one of several instances in which the libretto cites sexual instinct as a valid guide to human behavior. As Hilarion initially prepares to pursue his reluctant bride, he gathers his friends around him:

(217)

Come, Cyril, Florian, our course is plain,
    To-morrow morn fair Ida we'll engage;
But we will use no force her love to gain,
    Nature has armed us for the war we wage!

In other words, a man need only follow his instincts if he would know the way to woo and win a woman. And the impulsion of Nature's mating call is lauded by the entire company in the opera's final chorus:

(235)

It were profanity
For poor humanity
To treat as vanity
    The sway of Love!
In no locality
Or principality
Is our mortality
    Its sway above!

Princess Ida thus closes on a genuflection to the sex drive.

Here, then, Gilbert imprudently forced upon his audience's attention the issue of Nature's moral reliability. If science had led educated Victorians to conceive Nature as a force "indifferent to all moral values, impelling all things to a life of instinctive cruelty," the high Savoy operas rarely affirm that instinct ought to be trusted. But in *Princess Ida,* it is repeatedly invoked in the justifications that the various characters offer for their actions and attitudes. The Darwinian resonances of such rationales would have been especially audible in Melissa's response to Florian, coming as it does almost immediately after Psyche's song about "Darwinian man" had attuned the audience's ears to the subject. And they must have become positively deafening in the opera's final scene, which blares forth the very issue that Gilbert so carefully avoided in the other high Savoy operas. Traditional comedy may merely imply that sexual union ensures the perpetuation of the species; *Princess Ida* explicitly says so. Hildebrand asks Ida:

(234)

> If you enlist all women in your cause,
> And make them all abjure tyrannic Man,
> The obvious question then arises, "How
> Is this Posterity to be provided?"

The problem was, by 1884, this question no longer seemed purely rhetorical. Victorians had been given reason to doubt the existence of any viable long-range answer to it, and would therefore have probably preferred not to grapple with it at all. In general, Gilbert gratified this preference. In *Princess Ida* he neglected to do so, and this, I believe, may be why the opera achieved a run of only 246 performances—"in Gilbertian terms . . . a failure."[78]

III

Conclusion

GIVEN THE RADICAL DIFFERENCES between Gilbert's high Savoy operas and traditional "comedy," might another label more appropriately be affixed to them? Perhaps one may be inferred from the agenda that shaped and vitalized their comic dramaturgy: the glorification of law, of the status quo defined and maintained by law, and of the ideals of one particular social class. These were the aims of a writer of masques, and I propose that this was the true genre of the mature Savoy librettos. Gilbert's career, then, paralleled Ben Jonson's not only in his rejection of love as the central concern of comedy but also in his gradual movement away from "pure" comedy toward this more idealized form.

The settings of masque "are seldom remote from magic and fairy land, from Arcadias and visions of earthly Paradise," writes Frye—and we may note how frequently Gilbert transports us to the haunts and habitations of beings who are magical (in *Iolanthe*), supernatural (in *Ruddigore*), or at least exotic (in *The Pirates of Penzance, The Mikado,* and *Utopia*). "A female figure symbolizing some kind of reconciling unity and order appears dimly at the end of the great panoramic masques of *Faust* and *Peer Gynt*"; native English examples include Sabrina in Milton's *Comus* and the Moon in Jonson's *Masque of Blackness*. In Gilbert's work, the superintendence of such a reconciling female marks the final scenes of *The Pirates of Penzance,* in which the mention of "Queen Victoria's name" (134) moves the pirates to yield themselves to the law, and of *Utopia (Limited),* in which King Paramount and his formerly rebellious subjects join together to hymn the praises of a feminized Great Britain. And the structure of masque, Frye observes, is essentially the "processional structure" of "spectacular drama"; that is, its tendency is to present episodically a series of scenes which are not strongly linked to one another by the dramatic action.[1] Such a tendency is also present in the first acts of most Savoy operas, as the principal characters enter one by one to sing songs that introduce themselves but make no contribution whatever to the plot. *Pinafore* provides the most extreme example of this practice, as the sailors first sing one such number, Buttercup and the Captain each sing another, and Sir Joseph then sings two.

But these details alone do not qualify the operas as masques; indeed, many of these elements are also found in other comic forms. Rather, an essential commonality of purpose and perspective associates Gilbert's mature work with masque and distinguishes both from most traditional comedy. For while such comedy is "almost always destructive and anarchic, and . . . takes a position apart from morality and accepted standards," the masque enthusiastically and flatteringly subscribes to the established values of its audience; indeed, "it is usually a compliment to the audience . . . and leads up to an idealization of the society represented by that audience. . . . The ideal masque . . . is designed to emphasize, not the ideals to be achieved by discipline or faith, but ideals which are desired and considered to be already possessed." G. K. Chesterton holds that the Savoy operas were born of an era imbued with this very spirit of self-satisfaction—an era of "bourgeois Saturnalia," in which "Men believed that the consolidated commercial civilization of England, with its great wealth and its world-wide base, was already cast in a mould of manners and morals that could not really be shaken."[2] The newly ascendant social class celebrated its triumph, and Gilbert responded with comic plays that were little less than apotheoses of the written and unwritten laws in which that class's manners and morals were codified—plays that were, in short, middle-class masques.

Nor do the characters who populate these plays require "discipline or faith" or even Bergsonian ridicule in order to perfect their behavior: most evince a legalistic ethos from the first, showing that they—like the audiences whose self-image they reflect—have "already possessed" and internalized the ideals of Victorian society. The sins of their less numerous but more selfish colleagues tend to be benignly overlooked; very few are conspicuously unpardonable reprobates. Consequently, we notice in the high Savoy operas the

almost total absence of comedy's "scapegoat ritual of expulsion."
This is, of course, a favorite weapon of satirical comedy, but it also
appears in such gentler pieces as *Twelfth Night* and *As You Like It,*
where it is a punishment self-inflicted by Malvolio and Jaques. It
would, however, strike a distinctly discordant note among the
celebratory chords of masque: thus, such dubious Savoy characters
as Dick Deadeye, Lady Blanche, King Gama, Katisha, Dick Dauntless, Wilfred Shadbolt, and Grand Duke Rudolph are all present and
accepted at the festivities ending their operas, with the last four even
provided mates. Indeed, Gilbert chose to have the ritual of expulsion enacted in only two of his mature librettos—and even in these
instances, his prime objective remained the affirmation of English
bourgeois values. Sypher's comments define the spirit in which he
sighted his targets:

> One of the strongest impulses comedy can discharge from the depths
> of the social self is our hatred of the "alien," especially when the
> stranger who is "different" stirs any . . . doubt about our own
> beliefs. Then the comedian unerringly finds his audience, the solid
> majority, itself a silent prey to unrecognized fears. He can point out
> our victim, isolate him from our sympathy, and cruelly expose him
> to the penalty of our ridicule. In this role the comic artist is a
> "conservative" or even a "reactionary" who protects our self-
> esteem. . . . In middle-class societies, particularly, the comic artist
> often reassures the majority that its standards are impregnable or
> that other standards are not "normal" or "sane."

Thus, the aristocratic Bunthorne, who has taught the women's
chorus of *Patience* to despise the mundanity and materialism of
middle-class England ("He has come among us, and he has idealized us" [148]) and who, unlike his pupils, never publicly re-
nounces such attitudes, cannot be absorbed into the play's purified
final society; his "ultra-poetical, super-aesthetical, / Out-of-the-
way" values are simply antithetical to the "steady-and-stolid-y,
jolly bank-holiday" (164) ethos of the businesslike Victorian bourgeoisie. The last lines sung by the chorus explicitly deny him
comedy's standard reward:

(166)

> Greatly pleased with one another,
>   To get married we decide,
> Each of us will wed the other,
>   Nobody be Bunthorne's Bride!

As Ellis suggests, Gilbert "lets his audience feel that . . . it is their common sense which finally wins the day."[3] A similar, though more jingoistic, sense of vindication is made available by the finale of *Utopia (Limited),* as Scaphio and Phantis, who have raised an anti-English rebellion, are dragged off in custody, excluded from the happiness that Zara predicts her country will derive from following Britain's glorious example.

Indeed, despite its pointed jibes at certain flaws in English society, *Utopia* waxes well-nigh millennial in its exaltation of that society's institutions. Perry observes that Gilbert's

> *partial notion of perfection is aptly summed up in the title* Utopia (Limited). . . . *This apotheosis of an ideal state until it becomes "England—with improvements" is characteristically Gilbertian. It implies that England is not perfect as it is, but that it is progressing on the right track to a heaven upon earth. The absurdities of Victorian existence are only slightly caused by its falling short of what it might be; for the most part they depend upon minor deviations from the established order.*[4]

Specifically, Zara's final speech charges all the evils of English society to the account of Government by Party. Indeed, the successes heretofore achieved by her imported reformers add up to an argument that English institutions, if only more solidly based upon the business practices of the City (as explained and implemented by Mr. Goldbury) and protected from the depredations of party politics, would bring forth a perfect society; the only discontented citizens would be those who batten professionally upon human misery, such as the doctors who "dwindle, starve, and die" with no diseases to treat and the lawyers who likewise "starve" once "crime and litigation" have been "extinguished" (411). To be sure, Scaphio and Phantis successfully induce the Utopian populace to rebel against the bliss bestowed on them by English institutions, but this merely demonstrates the corruptibility of the human will, a phenomenon observed in similar circumstances by the authors of Genesis and *Paradise Lost*. And while the successor to *Utopia, The Grand Duke,* does not specifically champion the paradisaical institutions of Victorian England, it is no less a polemic on behalf of the status quo: the whole of its plot builds to the point that only the restoration of the rightful monarch—personally obnoxious though he may be—can bring order to the play's society and happiness to its sympathetic characters.

And if *Utopia* and *The Grand Duke* are especially enthusiastic about the ideality of the status quo, we should not be surprised that the original productions of these operas were so elaborately fitted with the trappings of masque—more so, perhaps, than any of their predecessors. Frye notes that "The further comedy moves from irony, and the more it rejoices in the free movement of its happy society, the more readily it takes to music and dancing. As music and scenery increase in importance, the ideal comedy crosses the boundary line of spectacular drama and becomes the masque." Music was not notably more important in the last two Savoy operas than it had been in the previous twelve (though there is somewhat more dance music); spectacle, on the other hand, certainly was. John Wolfson suggests that "Gilbert compensated for his insecurities as he rehearsed *Utopia (Limited)* by relying upon lavishness and sheer visual spectacle to a degree never before attempted at the Savoy." The scenery and costumes were remarkable through all the piece:

> But the most lavish of all Gilbert's effects was the Drawing Room Scene in Act II in which all of the members of the Utopian Court are presented to King Paramount in the exact manner of a Court presentation at Buckingham Palace. A parquet floor was built to cover the stage of the Savoy for the event. It took five costumiers to make the dresses worn by the ladies in that scene alone. Gilbert hired a female teacher of deportment to come to some of the rehearsals and teach the members of the cast how to walk, stand, and bow in the presence of royalty. Gilbert left no detail unattended in the

mounting of this scene, and no expense was spared. The effect was
totally visual—no dialogue was spoken in the entire scene.

Nor was the production of *The Grand Duke* less resplendent: "The
costumes were so impressive that they became the subject of an
entire article in *Sketch*," and the reviewer for the *Sunday Times* made
special note of "the magnificent mediaeval set."[5] Indeed, the librettos for these final operas seem merely pretexts for filling the
stage with two hours' worth of such entertainment, as Zara and the
Notary experience convenient first-act memory lapses (about Government by Party in the one case and the value of ace in the other)
which can be explained only by the need to prevent the plots from
being resolved too quickly.

And yet, despite their unabashed and unstinting celebrations of
middle-class values, neither *Utopia* nor *The Grand Duke* achieved a
run as long as the least successful of their high Savoy predecessors.
Many critics have traced this falling off to a corresponding de-
cline in quality: "The fact is the collaboration was past its artistic
height," says Williamson; "after twenty years, and understandably,
the fires of inspiration were burned out, freshness and vitality on
the wane."[6] But, defensible as this judgment may be, it is hardly a
statement of "fact"; it tells us, in any case, more about the responses
of the modern critic who subscribes to it than those of the audiences
who actually patronized, or determined to avoid, the Savoy Theatre in the 1890s. To understand their behavior, we must also
understand the new intellectual and ethical spirit that permeated the
people and playhouses of the last Victorian decade—and rendered
Gilbertian comedy an anachronism.

Rump steak with oyster sauce had not simply lost its savor.
Rather, any attempt "to supply a meal of one dish at which all
classes of the community are to sit down" was becoming increasingly futile. The once solid Victorian social consensus, with its
foundations in the values of the bourgeoisie, had finally begun to
crumble. One symptom of this process was the Aesthetic movement, which "ended the cultural parochialism which had been
one of the most deadening aspects of English life under Philistine
middle-class rule." Though this movement was well under way by

the eighties (when Gilbert lampooned it in *Patience*), its noncon-
formist spirit intensified and darkened in the following decade,
such that "the Decadence of the 'Yellow Nineties' is better regarded
as a separate, though derivative, phenomenon. . . . As a token
of their contempt for respectability, the Decadents extended the
Aesthetes' cultivation of the senses to the realm of the abnormal and
perverse (according to the prevailing moral standards): sexual aber-
rations, drug-taking, absinthe-drinking—an array of vices sufficient to rend the whole massive monolith of Victorian morality."
Their behavior, of course, never became that of mainstream Victorian society. Indeed, many among the stolid bourgeoisie shored
up their defenses to resist the attack on their value system, but their
responses tended toward simpleminded emotionalism. Thus we
find a regression into pietistic melodrama—examples are Wilson
Barrett's *The Sign of the Cross* (1895) and Hall Caine's *The Christian*
(1899)—and thus we also encounter the aggressive jingoism which
became one of the uglier political features of Victoria's final decade.
But the more thoughtful among the middle class did not shut their
ears to the Aesthetic critique of their way of life, and the result
was that "The rigidity of the earlier generations gave way before
a newer generation's repugnance for 'respectability.' Freedom in
thought and belief, the conviction that all is relative, and that life is
for the living, followed naturally on the earlier wave of agnosticism. . . . In the relaxed mood created by the aesthetes, by Pater,
Swinburne, and FitzGerald's Omar, the late-Victorian saw the
imminent dissolution of the sturdy world of his fathers."[7] In such a
climate, the reverence for law which had been the soul of Gilbert's
Savoy comedy was, like the style of comedy itself, doomed. And so
we have a somewhat bitter final parallel between Jonson and Gilbert: though the former was recognized in his later years as England's first Poet Laureate, and the latter became the first dramatist
to be knighted for services to the theater, both outlived the prime of
their popularity on the English stage.

The radical shift in audience consciousness is ironically illustrated by the popularity that playwrights of the nineties derived
from working with themes and character types that had earned
Gilbert the public's displeasure in the seventies. For instance, when

Arthur Wing Pinero produced *The Second Mrs. Tanqueray* in 1893, he achieved a triumph in spite of—perhaps even because of—his boldness in not only encouraging sympathy for a "fallen woman" but also in venturing "to criticize the 'dual morality' which its audience held dear. . . . it was the 'man with a past' whom Pinero judged and condemned." Yet Gilbert had done little less in *Charity* (1874), which favorably portrays two fallen women: Mrs. Van Brugh, the very personification of the title; and Ruth Tredgett, seduced at sixteen by a hypocrite who now condemns her in the same breath in which he cites his "extreme youth" to excuse himself ("I was barely forty then"). The time, however, was not yet ripe for such a piece: as Kate Field wrote in 1879, " 'the great big stupid,' as Thackeray called the public, refused to take its daughters to such an iniquitous exhibition," and *Charity* was "withdrawn after the eightieth night."[8]

Two years after *Mrs. Tanqueray,* Oscar Wilde scored his greatest theatrical hit with *The Importance of Being Earnest*—a piece which has been shown to be more than a little indebted to Gilbert's *Engaged* (1877) for details of situation, tone, and, especially, characterization.[9] Lighter in mood than Pinero's but no friendlier to the bourgeoisie, Wilde's play took particular pleasure in exposing the falseness of middle-class sentimentality: its high-sounding speeches are merely and clearly coverings for the vanity motivating the romantic protestations of Gwendolen and Cecily, the self-regarding snobbery underpinning Lady Bracknell's maternal solicitude, the callous lust behind Algernon's actions, and the two-faced hypocrisy behind Jack's. However, while theatergoers of the mid-nineties may have delighted in Wilde's derisive etchings, their counterparts of the mid-seventies had responded rather differently to Gilbert's collection of characters whose greed and lust are similarly visible beneath their sentimental diction: *Engaged,* as previously noted, was loudly condemned by the critics and bettered the run of *Charity* by only twenty-five performances.

A final example is provided by the fortunes of Shaw's *John Bull's Other Island* (1904), a play with close parallels to Gilbert's *Topsyturvydom* (1874). Both feature an English Member of Parliament as protagonist (in Gilbert's play he is already in the Commons, while in Shaw's we see him elected to the House), and both depict his journey to a strange land with a very different way of life. Each of the dramatists clearly implies that this journey ought to spur the Englishman to a reexamination of his most fundamental values, but each of the protagonists proves smugly impervious to such a notion, bumptiously bears all before him, and ultimately brings away a bride from the country he has visited. But while Gilbert's satire on his countrymen's unshakable self-satisfaction lasted barely a month on stage, Shaw's was graced with what amounted to official approval: in 1905, Edward VII attended a command performance at the Court Theatre, and, five years later, a single act of the play was performed at 10 Downing Street as part of the festivities for George V's coronation.[10]

After watching others succeed where his own early efforts had failed, Gilbert also lived to see the chief dramaturgical postulates of his mature comedy rejected by the most important plays of his final decade's most important playwrights. If the high Savoy plots revolve happily around law, John Galsworthy's *Justice* (1910) assigned the same centrality to the same force but showed the agents of this law hounding the pitiful Falder to his death, even after he has served his sentence in prison. If Gilbert honored the bourgeoisie, treated fathers with respect, and established submissiveness to law as the prevailing ethos among his characters, Granville-Barker's *The Voysey Inheritance* (1905) presented a middle-class lawyer whose legacy to his sons is a tangled web of corrupt business dealings, which some of his heirs are perfectly ready to conceal and even to continue weaving. And if Gilbert attempted to soothe his audience's anxieties about the perpetuity of the species by subordinating his juvenile love plots and downplaying the procreative implications of marriage, Shaw unblinkingly confronted Darwinism and, as Knight observes, made its principles central to his comedy, where "His considered philosophy is evolutionary. He believes in the Life Force, affirming an optimistic recognition of its miraculous nature as it travails to create a greater humanity, of which certain great men of history are the precursors. Its power is strong in women, who are impelled by it, as *Man and Superman* . . . shows, to win a husband and bear children."[11] Thus, Ann's pursuit of Tanner dominates the action of this play, and her triumphant capture of him concludes it.

Nor were early twentieth-century audiences either affrighted or offended by Shaw's explicit affirmation of evolution: rather, *Man and Superman* was "by far the most popular" of the plays produced during the 1904–7 Vedrenne-Barker management of the Court Theatre.[12]

Shaw's success puts Gilbert's in perspective. Seen from the viewpoint of cultural history, Gilbert's dramaturgical attempt to evade the conclusions of science could never have amounted to more than a rearguard action in the reluctant Victorian retreat from moral and religious certainty; clearly, the field—and the future of comedy—had inevitably to be possessed by those dramatists who "undertook to grapple with the new scientific thought and its revelations of man's nature and ways."[13] To the rising playwrights of the nineties, this future was revealed in the works of Ibsen, made available to English readers in the eighties by William Archer's translations and to English theatergoers in 1891 by J. T. Grein's Independent Theatre. To be sure, the "new drama," with its pointed social criticism, did not immediately capture the public's fancy: Clement Scott, the leading critic of the day, denounced Grein's first production, *Ghosts,* as "an open drain," "a loathsome sore unbandaged," "a dirty act done publicly," and "a lazar-house with all its doors and windows open,"[14] and the Independent Theatre remained an unprofitable venture throughout the whole of the nineties.[15] But, like the Aesthetes who lived on the fringe of English society but made their presence felt at its center, the influence of the Ibsenites emanated throughout the theatrical establishment: they affected the development of Pinero, a writer of farce and romantic comedy until he made a "careful study" of the Norwegian master's work,[16] and they launched the career of Shaw, whose first play, *Widowers' Houses,* was produced by Grein in 1892, and whose subsequent efforts proved popular enough to earn him a measure of financial security within the next four years.[17] Gradually, then, the nineties evolved into what Newell Sawyer calls "a decade of criticism and of protest against the moral inhibitions of puritanism and the banalities of philistinism," as the patronage of even respectable theatergoers was diverted to drama in which "Society becomes the villain of the play."[18]

In such an atmosphere, the pro-social comedy of the high

Savoy operas must have seemed as outmoded as plays making vigorous defenses of the fallen woman do today. Shaw was one of the first to denigrate Gilbert's comic method as inimical to the new drama's values: writing in 1891 as if the subject of his discourse were already a part of the theatrical past, the younger man claimed that Gilbert

> could always see beneath the surface of things; and if he could only have seen through them, he might have made his mark as a serious dramatist instead of having, as a satirist, to depend for the piquancy of his ridicule on the general assumption of the validity of the very things he ridiculed. The theme of The Pirates of Penzance is essentially the same as that of Ibsen's Wild Duck; but we all understand that the joke of the pirate being "the slave of duty" lay in the utter absurdity and topsyturviness of such a proposition, whereas when we read The Wild Duck we see that the exhibition of the same sort of slave as a mischievous fool is no joke at all, but a grimly serious attack on our notion that we need stick at nothing in the cause of our duty.

Of course, with *The Gondoliers* having completed one of the most successful runs in the Savoy series less than three weeks before Shaw wrote these words, Gilbert can hardly have been expected to realize that the tide of the public's consciousness was turning; indeed, his popularity to date had been predicated upon his refusal to challenge "the general assumption of the validity of the very things he ridiculed" or to attack "our notion that we need stick at nothing in the cause of our duty." But the gospel that had been so eagerly received by patrons of *Pirates* in 1880 proved less acceptable to the nineties. "The old melodrama and comic opera," writes Nicoll, "were ceasing to have their earlier appeal; the public was now clamouring for realism." Indeed, by 1894, a writer for *The Theatre* (the leading journal of the London stage) was referring to the drama of 1878 as "prehistoric."[19] And we might note that one of the most outstanding theatrical triumphs of the 1878 season had been *H.M.S. Pinafore*, while one of the great disappointments of 1894 was *Utopia (Limited)*, which closed on June 9 of that year after a run of just 245 performances.

Thus, my hypothesis is that, no matter how fresh, witty, or musically sparkling *Utopia* or *The Grand Duke* might have been, their comic dramaturgy would have doomed them to failure in the nineties. Nor did their predecessors now fare much better: of the eight older Gilbert and Sullivan operas revived by D'Oyly Carte during this decade, only *The Mikado*—which ran for 353 performances in 1895–97, interrupted by the short-lived *Grand Duke*—achieved a longer run than *Utopia;* none of the others reached even 200 performances.[20] Meanwhile, critics in sympathy with the new drama began to scoff at the operas as relics of the past; Augustin Filon, for instance, wrote in 1897 that "The English owe a debt of gratitude to their compatriots for having dethroned burlesque and operetta, two imports from France which competed with the national manufacture. So far so well, but I doubt whether the native comic opera will survive its originators. Already they are out of fashion. For my part, I never yawned so much as I did at *Princess Ida,* unless it was at *Patience*."[21]

Gilbert, for his part, refused to accept or adapt to the new dispensation. Though he spoke respectfully of Pinero in an 1897 interview with the *Edinburgh Evening Dispatch*,[22] Pearson asserts that he "never liked the advanced drama, whether French, German, Norwegian, or British."[23] In 1909, he revealed his antagonism toward the thematic content of such drama when he testified before a Joint Parliamentary Committee that he favored censorship "Because I think that the stage is not a proper pulpit from which to disseminate doctrines of anarchism, socialism, and agnosticism. It is not the proper platform upon which to discuss questions of adultery and free love before a mixed audience."[24] But perhaps the most telling evidence of his attitude consisted in the kind of plays he continued to write. In 1904, when Gilbert produced *The Fairy's Dilemma,* Max Beerbohm expressed his opinion that "the whole play should have been in verse." However, "verse is not the only thing that it ought to have been written in," declared Beerbohm. "It ought also to have been written in the seventies."[25]

Notes

Index

Notes

I: Introduction

1. Isaac Goldberg, *The Story of Gilbert and Sullivan or, The "Compleat" Savoyard* (New York: Simon, 1928), 222.
2. Raymond Mander and Joe Mitchenson, *The Theatres of London* (London: Rupert Hart-Davis, 1961), 177. The term "Savoy operas" used throughout this study as a short form of reference to all fourteen of the stage works on which Gilbert and Sullivan collaborated is partially a misnomer. Only eight of these works actually premiered at the Savoy, though all but one of the earlier six were revived at the theater during the authors' lifetimes. Given the house's association with virtually the whole of the Gilbert and Sullivan canon, the "Savoy" label has traditionally been affixed to all the operas written by them.
3. See Allardyce Nicoll, *A History of Late Nineteenth Century Drama, 1850–1900*, 2 vols. (Cambridge: Cambridge Univ. Press, 1946), 1:160–61.
4. W. S. Gilbert, letter to Arthur Sullivan, 19 February 1888, in Arthur Jacobs, *Arthur Sullivan: A Victorian Musician* (Oxford: Oxford Univ. Press, 1984), 265.
5. W. S. Gilbert, "An Autobiography," *The Theatre* ns 1 (1883), rpt. in *W. S. Gilbert: A Century of Scholarship and Commentary*, ed. John Bush Jones (New York: New York Univ. Press, 1970), 52.
6. See "Gilbert and Sullivan," *Fortune* (Feb. 1937): 101–2.
7. Herman Pückler-Muskau, *Tour in England, Ireland, and France, in the Years 1826, 1827, 1828, and 1829* (Philadelphia, 1833), excerpted and rpt. as "Turbulent Audiences," in *A Source Book in Theatrical History (Sources of Theatrical History)*, ed. A. M. Nagler (1952; New York: Dover, 1959), 476; Nicoll, *Late Nineteenth Century Drama*, 1:8.
8. Charles E. Grigsby, "When Gilbert and Sullivan Began," *Gilbert and Sullivan Journal* (1927), quoted in Leslie Baily, *The Gilbert and Sullivan Book* (London: Cassell, 1952), 102; Richard D. Altick, *Victorian People and Ideas* (New York: Norton, 1973), 184.
9. E. J. Hobsbawm, *Industry and Empire: From 1750 to the Present Day*, vol. 3 of *The Pelican Economic History of Britain* (1968; Harmondsworth: Penguin, 1977), 155; Michael R. Booth, ed., Introduction, *English Plays of the Nineteenth Century*, 5 vols. (Oxford: Clarendon-Oxford Univ. Press, 1969), 1:5–6, 1:6; Nicoll, *Late Nineteenth Century Drama*, 1:8–9.
10. Douglas Jerrold, rev. of *On Theatrical Emancipation and the Rights of Dramatists*, by T. J. Thackeray, *The New Monthly Magazine* (May 1832), rpt. as "The English Stage—1832," in Blanchard Jerrold, *The Life and Remains of Douglas Jerrold* (Boston: Ticknor and Fields, 1859), 415; Newell W. Sawyer, *The Comedy of Manners from Sheridan to Maugham* (Philadelphia: Univ. of Pennsyl-

vania Press, 1931), 32; George Rowell, *The Victorian Theatre, 1792–1914,* 2nd ed. (Cambridge: Cambridge Univ. Press, 1978), 64.

11. See Sidney Dark and Rowland Grey, *W. S. Gilbert: His Life and Letters* (London: Methuen, 1923), 196; W. S. Gilbert, letter to Arthur Coke, 3 July 1907, in Dark and Grey, *W. S. Gilbert,* 197.

12. Rowell, *Victorian Theatre,* 163.

13. Allardyce Nicoll, *A History of Early Nineteenth Century Drama, 1800–1850,* 2 vols. (Cambridge: Cambridge Univ. Press, 1930), 1:52.

14. Nicoll, *Late Nineteenth Century Drama,* 1:69.

15. See Nicoll, *Late Nineteenth Century Drama,* 1:68.

16. W. S. Gilbert, Speech at the O. P. Club, London, 30 December 1906, rpt. in Dark and Grey, *W. S. Gilbert,* 194.

17. Rowell, *Victorian Theatre,* 165.

18. See [Colin Prestige], "Ourselves and the Operas: Random Notes by the Editor," *Gilbert and Sullivan Journal* 10 (1973): 27.

19. See Townley Searle, *A Bibliography of Sir William Schwenck Gilbert, with Bibliographical Adventures in the Gilbert and Sullivan Operas* (London: n.p., 1931), 30.

20. Hobsbawm, *Industry and Empire,* 127, 128.

21. Hobsbawm, *Industry and Empire,* 157.

22. See Nicoll, *Late Nineteenth Century Drama,* 1:8.

23. See Richard Fawkes, *Dion Boucicault: A Biography* (London: Quartet, 1979), 72.

24. See Jane W. Stedman, ed., Introduction, *Gilbert Before Sullivan: Six Comic Plays by W. S. Gilbert* (Chicago: Univ. of Chicago Press, 1967), 1, 3–5, 9.

25. Rowell, *Victorian Theatre,* 83.

26. On the sizes of these four theaters, see Diana Howard, *London Theatres and Music Halls, 1850–1950* (London: Library Association, 1970), 90, 216, 167, and 214 respectively. (On the Prince of Wales's, cf. the Introduction in William Tydeman, ed., *Plays by Tom Robertson,* British and American Playwrights, 1750–1920 [Cambridge: Cambridge Univ. Press, 1982], which observes that, while Howard gives the capacity of the theater as circa 600, "her breakdown [stalls 143; pit 85; gallery 134; boxes 142] suggests a figure nearer 500" [29n]). Both the Reeds and the Bancrofts eventually rode the rising tide of middle-class patronage to larger theaters: the former moved to the 1,000-seat St. George's Hall in 1875, while the latter took over the newly reconstructed 1,159-seat Haymarket in 1880 (see Howard, *London Theatres,* 210 and 109 respectively).

27. W. S. Gilbert, letter to Richard D'Oyly Carte, 1882, in Baily, *G + S Book,* 205.

28. On the monetary value of a full house at the Savoy, see Dark and Grey, *W. S. Gilbert,* 85. On the takings of the Drury Lane, see Booth, Introduction, *English Plays,* 1:5; on its size, see Howard, *London Theatres,* 66.

29. See "Gilbert and Sullivan," *Fortune,* 102.

30. See Reginald Allen, ed., *The First Night Gilbert and Sullivan: Containing Complete Librettos of the Fourteen Operas, Exactly as Presented at Their Premiere Performances,* by W. S. Gilbert, Centennial ed. (London: Chappell, 1975). In his

introductions to *Patience* (the piece that was transferred from the Opera Comique in 1881 for the opening of the Savoy) and to all the eight subsequent Gilbert and Sullivan operas, Allen lists the celebrities in attendance at each first night—including royalty, nobility, businessmen, philanthropists, politicians, and jurists—and quotes the testimony of contemporary reviewers to the brilliance of these audiences. And while the audiences for the later performances in each run may not have featured as many *illuminati*, their regular presence at the premieres continually reaffirmed that the Savoy was a theater in which respectable Victorians need not fear to tread. See also Regina Kirby Higgins, "Victorian Laughter: The Comic Operas of Gilbert and Sullivan" (Ph.D. diss., Indiana University, 1985), 4, for a convincing argument that neither the aristocracy nor the working class was "well represented" in the average Savoy audience: its bulk was bourgeois.

31. Goldberg, *Story of G + S*, 189–90; Ilka von Palmay, *Meine Erinnerungen* (Berlin, 1911), excerpted as "At the Savoy Theatre," trans. Andrew Lamb, *Gilbert and Sullivan Journal* 9 (1972): 417.

32. Dion Boucicault, letter to Marie Bancroft, 1868, in Squire and Marie Bancroft, *Mr. and Mrs. Bancroft On and Off the Stage*, 4th ed., 2 vols. (London, 1888), 1:245–46.

33. On the nineteenth-century bourgeoisie's receptivity to comedy, cf. Roger B. Henkle, *Comedy and Culture: England 1820–1900* (Princeton: Princeton Univ. Press, 1980). Henkle claims, very defensibly, that the Victorian "atmosphere . . . was one in which comic prose flourished as never before"; still, he admits that it "was apparently uncongenial to original comic theatre" (5). To some extent, the solution to this paradox might be that the respectable middle classes were unwilling publicly to patronize the playhouses' presentation of the same material by which they permitted themselves to be privately amused at home. But we have reason to doubt whether the "comic prose" most enthusiastically embraced by the bourgeoisie truly embodied the principles and prejudices that are traditional to comedy: see the arguments of Christopher Herbert and D. A. Miller, cited below.

34. Nicoll, *Early Nineteenth Century Drama*, 1:15; Edward Bulwer-Lytton, Baron Lytton, *Dramatic Works* (London, 1841), quoted in Nicoll, *Late Nineteenth Century Drama*, 1:120; Christopher Herbert, *Trollope and Comic Pleasure* (Chicago: Univ. of Chicago Press, 1987), 3, 4.

35. Northrop Frye, "The Problem of Spiritual Authority in the Nineteenth Century," *Essays in English Literature from the Renaissance to the Victorian Age Presented to A. S. P. Woodhouse*, ed. Millar MacLure and F. W. Watt (Toronto: Univ. of Toronto Press, 1964), 305–6; Thomas Carlyle, *The Bastille*, Vol. 1 of *The French Revolution*, 2 vols., *Complete Works of Thomas Carlyle* (New York: Collier, 1901), Book 10, Chapter 1, 380.

36. Matthew Arnold, *Culture and Anarchy, Poetry and Criticism of Matthew Arnold*, ed. A. Dwight Culler (Boston: Houghton, 1961) Chapter 2, 429.

37. David Thomson, *England in the Nineteenth Century: 1815–1914*, Vol. 8 of *The Pelican History of England* (1950; Harmondsworth: Penguin, 1970), 181; Hobsbawm, *Industry and Empire*, 140.

38. Charles Frederick Harrold and William D. Templeman, eds., "Introductory

Survey: Major Aspects of the Victorian Period," *English Prose of the Victorian Era* (1938; New York: Oxford Univ. Press, 1968), lxix; Walter E. Houghton, *The Victorian Frame of Mind, 1830–1870* (1957; New Haven: Yale Univ. Press, 1974), 184; Altick, *Victorian People*, 175.

39. See Altick, *Victorian People*, 168–71 on the bourgeois blending of Utilitarianism and Evangelicalism, and on the importance to the latter of self-denial.

40. Nicoll, *Early Nineteenth Century Drama*, 1:18.

41. Northrop Frye, *Anatomy of Criticism: Four Essays* (1957; Princeton: Princeton Univ. Press, 1971), 163. Frye here asserts that this pattern, "in itself less a form than a formula, has become the basis for most comedy, especially in its more highly conventionalized dramatic form, down to our own day." His classic analysis of this formula has provided the basis for my own description of traditional comedy's anti-legal tendencies.

42. Susanne K. Langer, *Feeling and Form: A Theory of Art* (New York: Scribner's, 1953), 342, 343.

43. Frye, *Anatomy*, 181, 169; Maurice Charney, *Comedy High and Low: An Introduction to the Experience of Comedy* (New York: Oxford Univ. Press, 1978), 77–78.

44. Charney, *Comedy*, 170–71; Frye, *Anatomy*, 172.

45. Houghton, *Victorian Frame of Mind*, 276; Langer, *Feeling and Form*, 343, 342.

46. Northrop Frye, *A Natural Perspective: The Development of Shakespearean Comedy and Romance* (New York: Columbia Univ. Press, 1965) 75–76; Frye, *Anatomy*, 173, 165.

47. Langer, *Feeling and Form*, 333, 349–50; Frye, *Anatomy*, 164.

48. Altick, *Victorian People*, 111–12; Charles Lyell, *Principles of Geology, Being an Attempt to Explain the Former Changes of the Earth's Surface, by Reference to Causes Now in Operation*, 3 vols. (London, 1830–33), 2:168–69; Alfred, Lord Tennyson, *In Memoriam*, ed. Robert H. Ross (New York: Norton, 1973), 35; 56.1–4.

49. Altick, *Victorian People*, 226, notes that Darwin did not introduce the phrase "survival of the fittest" until the 1872 edition of this book, but the concepts behind the phrase were surely present in 1859.

50. Frye, *Anatomy*, 170; *Natural Perspective*, 124–25.

51. *The Works of John Ruskin*, ed. E. T. Cook and Alexander Wedderburn, 39 vols. (London: George Allen, 1903–12), 36:115; William Irvine, *Apes, Angels, and Victorians: The Story of Darwin, Huxley, and Evolution* (New York: Time, 1955), 305, 6; Altick, *Victorian People*, 233.

52. Frye, *Anatomy*, 164.

53. Henri Bergson, *Laughter*, no trans. (1900), in *Comedy*, ed. Wylie Sypher (Garden City: Anchor-Doubleday, 1956) 64–65.

54. D. A. Miller, *The Novel and the Police* (Berkeley: Univ. of California Press, 1988), 17, 16.

55. Miller, *The Novel*, 9, 10.

56. Herbert, *Trollope*, 14, 34–35.

57. Booth, Introduction, *English Plays*, 5:6, 5:46; Hilary Thompson, "The Gilbertian Dame," *Savoyard* 14, no. 2 (1975): 18.

58. Harley Granville-Barker, "Exit Planché—Enter Gilbert," in *The Eighteen-Sixties: Essays by Fellows of the Royal Society of Literature*, ed. John Drinkwater (Cambridge: Cambridge Univ. Press, 1932), 106–7.

59. G. Wilson Knight, *The Golden Labyrinth: A Study of British Drama* (New York: Norton, 1962), 241.

60. All quotations from Gilbert's Savoy librettos are from *The First Night Gilbert and Sullivan*. Relevant page numbers for each quotation are given parenthetically in the text.

61. See Allen, "Encore: The First Nights of the First Revivals," *First Night Gilbert and Sullivan,* 456.

62. Alan S. Downer, *The British Drama: A Handbook and Brief Chronicle* (New York: Appleton, 1950), 274.

63. Rowell, *Victorian Theatre,* 83.

64. For less and more recent expressions of this view, see A. H. Godwin, *Gilbert and Sullivan* (1926; Port Washington: Kennikat, 1969), 31–33, and Peter Sellars, "Why Gilbert and Sullivan Endure," *Dial* (March 1984): 14–15. For a dissenting view, which accords with my own, see Goldberg, *Story of G + S,* 483–86.

65. J. R. Planché, Appendix, *The Extravaganzas of J. R. Planché, Esq.: 1825–1871,* ed. T. F. Dillon Croker and Stephen Tucker, 5 vols. (London, 1879), 1:286; Rowell, *Victorian Theatre,* 67; Ernest Reynolds, *Early Victorian Drama (1830–1870)* (1936; New York: Benjamin Blom, 1965), 69.

66. Arthur Sullivan, letter to Richard D'Oyly Carte, 26 March 1889, in Baily, *G + S Book,* 304.

67. Allen, Prologue, *First Night Gilbert and Sullivan,* xvi; Arthur Sullivan, letter to W. S. Gilbert, 12 March 1889, in Jacobs, *Arthur Sullivan,* 283.

68. Goldberg, *Story of G + S,* 64; Jane W. Stedman, "JW: G + S," *Gasbag* 14, no. 12 (1983): 13; Hesketh Pearson, *Gilbert: His Life and Strife* (London: Methuen, 1957), 62.

69. Mrs. Alec Tweedie, *My Table-Cloths; A Few Reminiscences* (New York: George H. Doran, 1916), 45; W. S. Gilbert, letter to Alfred Austin, 14 December 1889, in Allen, Introduction to *The Gondoliers, First Night Gilbert and Sullivan,* 346; "Gilbert and Sullivan," *Fortune,* 192.

70. W. S. Gilbert, "Collaborating with Sir Arthur Sullivan: A Chat with Mr. W. S. Gilbert," *Cassell's Saturday Journal* 21 March 1894, rpt. in *Savoyard* 16, no. 2 (1977): 32; W. S. Gilbert, interview, *Musical World* 14 March 1885, quoted in Brian Jones, "The Sword That Never Fell," *W. S. Gilbert Society Journal* 1 (1985): 24.

71. See Pearson, *Gilbert,* 40; James Delmont Ellis, "The Comic Vision of W. S. Gilbert" (diss., State Univ. of Iowa, 1964), 34.

II: The High Savoy Operas

1. W. S. Gilbert, letter to Mrs. Bram Stoker, 16 September 1904, in Reginald Allen, *W. S. Gilbert: An Anniversary Survey and Exhibition Checklist* (Charlottesville: Bibliographical Society of Univ. of Virginia, 1963), 76–77; see Goldberg, *Story of G + S,* 473.

2. See W. J. Macqueen-Pope, *Theatre Royal, Drury Lane* (London: W. H. Allen, 1945), 283.

3. W. S. Gilbert, "On Pantomimic Unities," *Fun* (20 February 1864): 230; "The Physiognomist at the Play," *Fun* (16 January 1864): 181.

4. W. S. Gilbert, *Foggerty's Fairy, Original Plays: Third Series* (1895; London: Chatto, 1928) 31–32. Gilbert's attitude toward pantomime never changed. As late as 1900, he resumed his indictment of its antisocial values in a prose tale entitled "The Fairy's Dilemma," which later became the basis for one of his last plays.

5. Goldberg, *Story of G + S,* 161; Granville-Barker, "Exit Planché," 145; Friedrich Dürrenmatt, *Problems of the Theatre,* trans. Gerhard Nelhaus (Grove, 1964), excerpted and rpt. as "From *Problems of the Theatre,*" in Robert W. Corrigan, ed., *Comedy: Meaning and Form,* 2nd ed. (New York: Harper, 1981), 133–34.

6. Gilbert, "Autobiography," 52; Lord Elwyn-Jones, Foreword, *Gilbert and Sullivan at Law* by Andrew Goodman (Rutherford: Fairleigh Dickinson Univ. Press, 1983), 9. Goodman notes that, throughout his life, Gilbert "kept up-to-date in all matters of legal topicality" (28).

7. Max Keith Sutton, *W. S. Gilbert,* Twayne's English Authors Series 178 (Boston: Twayne, 1975), 19. For an opinion concurring with Sutton's, see Jay Newman, "Gilbert and the Utilitarians," *Savoyard* 16, no. 2 (1977): 13–14. For an able refutation of Newman, see Phyllis Karr, " 'Gilbert and the Utilitarians' Revisited," *Gasbag* 10, no. 3 (1978): 21–22.

8. Ellis, "Comic Vision," 159–60. The context of Ellis's comments is a discussion of the quintet "Here is a case unprecedented" in *The Gondoliers;* I do not believe that I am misrepresenting his ideas when I suggest that his remarks apply to the pattern he perceives in the Savoy operas in general.

9. Lane Cooper, *An Aristotelian Theory of Comedy, With an Adaptation of the Poetics and a Translation of the "Tractatus Coislinianus"* (New York: Harcourt, 1922), 305.

10. Kim A. Emmence, "*Iolanthe* Legalities," *Gilbert and Sullivan Journal* 9 (1972): 442. Cf. Godwin, *Gilbert and Sullivan,* who more generally observes that "following a specious line of argument" is Gilbert's "favourite way of putting an end to the operas" (90).

11. For an analysis of the constituent parts of a syllogism and a summary of the rules governing its form and content, see John Stuart Mill, *A System of Logic,* 7th ed., 2 vols. (London, 1868), 1:184–86. This frequently reissued work would have been readily available, and possibly familiar, to Gilbert; at any rate, it may be regarded as an authoritative expression of the Victorian understanding of deductive logic.

12. Aristotle, *Poetics* 24, in Cooper, *Aristotelian Theory,* 217.

13. Sypher, Introduction, in *Comedy,* x; Bergson, *Laughter,* 66–67, 148.

14. Jane W. Stedman, "William S. Gilbert: His Comic Techniques and Their Development" (diss., Univ. of Chicago, 1955), 190.

15. Allen, Introduction to *The Grand Duke, First Night Gilbert and Sullivan,* 418; Audrey Williamson, *Gilbert and Sullivan Opera: A New Assessment,* 2nd ed. (London: Rockliff, 1955), 103.

16. A. F. Marshall, "The Spirit of Gilbert's Comedies," *Month* 55 (1885): 262.

17. Ashley H. Thorndike, *English Comedy* (New York: Macmillan, 1929), 553. Of course, dissenters from this opinion exist. See Ellis, "Comic Vision," 75–78, for a survey of the critical views expressed on this issue up to 1964. The debate

has continued over the past quarter-century, with some critics endorsing the majority view (see, e.g., Christopher Hibbert, *Gilbert and Sullivan and Their Victorian World* [New York: American Heritage, 1976], 140) and an increasing number of others identifying Gilbert as a satirical enemy of his society's legalistic norms (see, e.g., Sutton, *W. S. Gilbert,* 21, and Charles Hayter, *Gilbert and Sullivan,* Modern Dramatists [New York: St. Martin's, 1987] 48–49).

18. Cooper, *Aristotelian Theory,* 69–70. Cooper infers Aristotle's philosophy of comedy from a variety of materials, including the fragmentary "Tractatus Coislinianus," which he believes to preserve "if not an original Aristotelian, at all events an early Peripatetic tradition" (13).

19. Sypher, Appendix: "The Meanings of Comedy," in *Comedy,* 199 and 222. Cf. the similar conception of the temporary release provided by comedy in C. L. Barber, *Shakespeare's Festive Comedy: A Study of Dramatic Form and Its Relation to Social Custom* (Princeton: Princeton Univ. Press, 1959), 7–8.

20. Frye, *Anatomy,* 170.

21. Houghton, *Victorian Frame of Mind,* 15.

22. Houghton, *Victorian Frame of Mind,* 68–69.

23. See Harrold and Templeman, *English Prose,* 1608n; John Stuart Mill, "Nature," from *Three Essays on Religion* (1874), in Harrold and Templeman, *English Prose,* 750–51.

24. Goldberg, *Story of G + S,* 173.

25. Jessie Bond, *The Life and Reminiscences of Jessie Bond, the Old Savoyard, As Told by Herself to Ethel Macgeorge* (London: Lane-Bodley Head, 1930) 64–65; Thorndike, *English Comedy,* 545.

26. Frye, *Anatomy,* 166.

27. Ellis, "Comic Vision," 177–78.

28. Frye, *Anatomy,* 169, 163.

29. Mill, *System of Logic,* 1:186, 254.

30. Frye, *Natural Perspective,* 123–24; *Anatomy,* 170–71.

31. Most notable of the critical commentaries on Gilbert's indebtedness to melodrama is Chapter 2 of Stedman, "William S. Gilbert," entitled "Gilbert's Relation to Victorian Melodrama," 137–97. See also Earl F. Bargainnier, "*Brantinghame Hall:* Gilbert as Melodramatist," *Gasbag* 11, no. 3 (1979): 19–22.

32. Stedman, "William S. Gilbert," 155.

33. W. S. Gilbert, *The Bab Ballads,* ed. James Ellis (1970; Cambridge: Belknap-Harvard Univ. Press, 1980) 93–94.

34. Stedman, "William S. Gilbert," 404–5.

35. Whether or not Point dies at the end of *Yeomen* has been the subject of some controversy, as the final stage direction simply indicates that "Point falls insensible" at the feet of the lovers (339). For a persuasive argument that Gilbert intended from the first that the final scene should be a death scene (as it is now usually played), see Gerald Glynn, "The Evidence for Thorne," *W. S. Gilbert Society Journal* 1 (1985): 9–12.

36. Northrop Frye, "Dickens and the Comedy of Humors," *Experience in the Novel: Selected Papers from the English Institute,* ed. Roy Harvey Pearce (New

York: Columbia Univ. Press, 1968); rpt. in *The Victorian Novel: Modern Essays in Criticism,* ed. Ian Watt (New York: Oxford Univ. Press, 1971), 50. For opposing views, see Sutton, *W. S. Gilbert,* 108, who finds in *Yeomen* "a final undertone of tragedy," and Jay Newman, "Dimensions of Gilbert's Comedy," *Gilbert and Sullivan Journal* 10 (1980): 382, who calls Point "a tragic figure."

37. Frye, *Natural Perspective,* 46.
38. Diana C. Burleigh, "A Point Little Considered," *Gilbert and Sullivan Journal* 8 (1965): 307.
39. Charney, *Comedy,* 172.
40. According to Leslie Baily, the playwright was unusually diligent in his research for this opera: "For months Gilbert was absorbed in Tudor England. He went to the Tower of London to sense its atmosphere, and to sketch its 'Beefeaters'" (*Gilbert and Sullivan: Their Lives and Times* [1973; Harmondsworth: Penguin, 1979], 92). The backdrop for the original production was a photographically accurate representation of the White Tower, and the costumes were impressively rich in period detail: see Robin Wilson and Frederic Lloyd, *Gilbert and Sullivan: The Official D'Oyly Carte Picture History* (New York: Knopf, 1984), 44–46.
41. W. S. Gilbert, letter to Arthur Sullivan, 20 February 1889, in Dark and Grey, *W. S. Gilbert,* 120–21.
42. See Williamson, *Gilbert and Sullivan,* 204–5.
43. "The Playhouses," rev. of *The Gondoliers, Illustrated London News* 14 Dec. 1889: 755.
44. George Meredith, "An Essay on Comedy" (1877), in *Comedy,* ed. Sypher, 13–14.
45. See "Criticism of *Engaged,*" in Booth, *English Plays,* 3:393.
46. Jim Davis, Introduction, *Plays by H. J. Byron,* British and American Playwrights, 1750–1920 (Cambridge: Cambridge Univ. Press 1984) 23. The reviews quoted by Davis emphasize the centrality of Middlewick to the appeal of the play.
47. H. J. Byron, *Our Boys,* in *Plays,* 158.
48. Nicoll, *Late Nineteenth Century Drama,* 1:22; Clement Scott, "Why Do We Go to the Play?" *The Theatre,* ns 11 (March 1888): 117–25.
49. Godwin, *Gilbert and Sullivan,* 35, 71; Stedman, Introduction, *Gilbert Before Sullivan,* 50.
50. Aristotle, *Poetics* 6, in Cooper, *Aristotelian Theory,* 185.
51. Phyllis Karr, "Gilbert's Little People," *Gasbag* 15, no. 5 (1984): 17.
52. Langer, *Feeling and Form,* 335; Charney, *Comedy,* 161.
53. An explanation of why I regard Paramount and Ludwig as the heroes of their operas seems in order. Taken as a general literary term, a "hero" is he whose actions shape the destiny of a nation or a race. In comedy, this function is somewhat domesticated, and the "hero" normally qualifies as such simply by joining with the heroine in a union which embodies the seeds of a new society; the "heroine," in turn, is such by virtue of those characteristics—such as youth and sexual desirability—which contribute to her reproductive potential. Given these definitions, however, the last two operas in the Savoy series

pose something of a problem. Though Zara is obviously the heroine of *Utopia (Limited)*, we do not know that Fitzbattleaxe will ever be her mate; indeed, a hint is given that the princess wishes to keep her relationship with this less-than-royal suitor a secret ("Words of love too loudly spoken," she warns him, "Ring their own untimely knell" [404]), and we never learn whether her father will approve of him as her husband. On the other hand, as Paramount is king of the island nation in which the action is set, and as it is upon his leadership that its people depend in transforming Utopia first into a "Monarchy (Limited)" and then into "what is a great deal better, a Limited Monarchy" (412), the indicators point to him as the play's most likely hero, despite his being the heroine's father rather than spouse. Likewise, in *The Grand Duke*, Ludwig's "heroic" status has mostly to do with him functioning as monarch, and therefore leader of his people, through most of the play. It has little to do with whom he marries, for Lisa, his eventual bride, is not clearly the heroine of the piece: as the soubrette of the Dummkopf acting troupe, she presumably possesses no more youth and beauty, and somewhat less prominence, than Julia, the company's leading lady.

54. Stedman, "William S. Gilbert," 154; Houghton, *Victorian Frame of Mind*, 248.
55. For the fragmentary text of Gilbert's early draft of *Patience* (derived from a British Museum manuscript) as well as Gilbert's statement about why he chose to change his clerics into aesthetes, see Jane W. Stedman, "The Genesis of *Patience*," *Modern Philology* 66 (1968), rpt. in *W. S. Gilbert: A Century of Scholarship*, 285–318.
56. George Rowell, Introduction, *Plays by W. S. Gilbert*, British and American Playwrights, 1750–1920 (Cambridge: Cambridge Univ. Press, 1982), 13.
57. Frye, *Anatomy*, 164–65.
58. Plato, *Philebus*, in *The Dialogues of Plato*, trans. B. Jowett, 3rd ed., 5 vols. (Oxford, 1892), 4:623.
59. Goldberg, *Story of G + S*, 171.
60. Cf., in *Trial By Jury*, the autobiographical song of the Judge who, like Sir Joseph, has risen from the ranks of the bourgeoisie. Unlike its equivalents in the high Savoy operas, this song does not deflect but rather invites the charge of hypocrisy, as the singer unrepentantly reveals the breach of promise he once committed against "a rich attorney's / Elderly, ugly daughter" (36), and then announces his readiness to try the present case, which involves the very same crime. If Gilbert's mature comedic agenda included flattery of the recently risen middle class and puffery of the law's representatives, that agenda was clearly not in place at the time he wrote *Trial By Jury*.
61. Earl F. Bargainnier, "*Ruddigore*: Gilbert's Burlesque of Melodrama," in *Gilbert and Sullivan: Papers Presented at the International Conference Held at the University of Kansas in May 1970*, ed. James Helyar (Lawrence: Univ. of Kansas Libraries, 1971), 14. For other negative views of Rose, see Godwin, *Gilbert and Sullivan*, 126, and Gervase Lambton, *Gilbertian Characters, and a Discourse on W. S. Gilbert's Philosophy in the Savoy Operas* (London: Allan, 1931), 94–97.
62. "Savoy Theatre," rev. of *Ruddygore*, *Times* (24 Jan. 1887): 4; W. S. Gilbert, Speech at the O. P. Club, in *Dark and Grey*, *W. S. Gilbert*, 194.

63. Stedman, "William S. Gilbert," 194; see Jacobs, *Arthur Sullivan,* 261.

64. Thorndike, *English Comedy,* 588; Corrigan, Introduction: "Comedy and the Comic Spirit," *Comedy: Meaning and Form,* 8.

65. Henry Ten Eyck Perry, "The Victorianism of W. S. Gilbert," *Sewanee Review* 36 (1928), rpt. in *W. S. Gilbert: A Century of Scholarship,* 151. For other suggestions that Gilbert was uninterested in writing about love, unable to write well about it, or simply cynical about romance and marriage, see Stedman, "William S. Gilbert," 402n; Augustin Filon, *The English Stage, Being an Account of the Victorian Drama,* trans. Frederic Whyte (1897; Port Washington: Kennikat, 1970), 141; and Goldberg, *Story of G + S,* 197. For dissenting views—which implicitly or explicitly maintain that love, marriage, and generation were thematically central to most of Gilbert's comedy—see Ellis, "Comic Vision," 270n; Albert Cook, *The Dark Voyage and the Golden Mean: A Philosophy of Comedy* (Cambridge: Harvard Univ. Press, 1949), 123; and J. D. McClure, "The Libretto of *The Mountebanks,*" *Savoyard* 18, no. 2 (1979): 15.

66. Phyllis Karr, "Ida and Hilarion and Robin and Rose," *Gasbag* 13, no. 4 (1982): 21.

67. Sutton, *W. S. Gilbert,* 98.

68. Arthur B. Brenner, "The Fantasies of W. S. Gilbert," *Psychoanalytic Quarterly* 21 (1952): 393.

69. *The Autobiography of Charles Darwin,* ed. Nora Barlow (London: Collins, 1958), 138, 139.

70. W. S. Gilbert, *His Excellency, Original Plays: Fourth Series* (1911; London: Chatto, 1924), 120.

71. Robert Flacelière, *Love in Ancient Greece,* trans. James Cleugh (1960; New York: Crown, 1962), 221, 220–21.

72. Rowell, *Victorian Theatre,* 69. Not all of Gilbert's contemporaries regarded Aristophanic comedy as distinct from the species I have labeled "traditional." In 1875, near the beginning of the high Savoy era, Browning published *Aristophanes' Apology,* in which the dramatist is presented as an exponent of instinctive and lawless energy:

> I praise the god
> Present in person of his minister,
> And pay—the wilder my extravagance—
> The more appropriate worship to the Power
> Adulterous, night-roaming, and the rest:
> Otherwise,—that originative force
> Of nature, impulse stirring death to life,
> Which, underlying law, seems lawlessness,
> Yet is the outbreak which, ere order be,
> Must thrill creation through, warm stocks
>   and stones,
> Phales Iacchos. Comedy for me!

(2357–67)

"Phales Iacchos" may be translated as "Phallic Bacchus" (Robert Browning, *The Poems,* ed. John Pettigrew and Thomas J. Collins, 2 vols. (New Haven:

Yale Univ. Press, 1981), 2:246–47, 1019n); he is, in Browning's view, the presiding genius of Aristophanes's plays. And he is clearly the presiding genius of Aubrey Beardsley's famous and scandalous illustrations to *Lysistrata* published in 1896, the year of *The Grand Duke*. These eight pornographic caricatures—of men with enormous erections and "Lysistrata Shielding Her Coynte"—obviously emphasize the erotic energy and tension of the play and thus suggest its affinities with traditional comedy (see *The Lysistrata of Aristophanes,* illus. Aubrey Beardsley [1973; London: Academy Editions, 1975]); however, as my own discussion of *Lysistrata* will suggest, its erotic content may be seen as subordinated in importance to other thematic concerns and the play thus construed as a model for Gilbert's high Savoy treatment of love.

73. W. S. Gilbert, *The Wicked World, Original Plays: First Series* (1876; London: Chatto, 1925), 3.

74. Sutton, *W. S. Gilbert,* 93. Sutton's treatment of the parallels between Gilbert and Aristophanes (see 88 ff.) seems to me the most substantive, and therefore most valuable, of the many attempts to compare and contrast these two dramatists. Among them may be noted: Walter Sichel, "The English Aristophanes," *Fortnightly Review* 96 (1911), and Edith Hamilton, "W. S. Gilbert: A Mid-Victorian Aristophanes," *Theatre Arts Monthly* 11 (1927), both rpt. in *W. S. Gilbert: A Century of Scholarship,* 69–109 and 111–34 respectively; Arthur M. Liebman, "The Works of W. S. Gilbert: A Study of Their Aristophanic Elements and Their Relation to the Development of the Nineteenth and Twentieth Century British Theatre" (Ph.D. diss., New York Univ. 1971); and R. W. Garson, "The English Aristophanes," *Revue de Littérature Comparée* 46 (1972): 177–93.

75. Thorndike, *English Comedy,* 588.

76. Both scenes are reprinted in John Wolfson, *Final Curtain: The Last Gilbert and Sullivan Operas* (London: Chappell, 1976), 195–201. Wolfson derives the texts from Gilbert's manuscript in the British Library. It is interesting also to note that, just days before the opening of the opera, Gilbert and Sullivan completely rewrote the finale, eliminating an affectionate exchange between the young lovers and thus depriving their relationship of any sort of closure: see Allen, Postscript to *Utopia (Limited), First Night G + S,* 414. This decision to edit out erotic closure is, moreover, in keeping with the anti-sexual imagery that Higgins culls from *Utopia.* "Zara the beautiful inspires passion," she observes, "but her lovers are frustrated by age and impotence": Scaphio speaks of his infatuation in terms of "convulsions, palsy, paralysis, and incoherence," while the underlying theme of Fitzbattleaxe's complaint that he cannot use his singing voice to express his love is, according to Higgins, "sexual incapacity" (see "Victorian Laughter," 170–72). She detects a similar failing of passionate love in *The Grand Duke,* noting that the word "tasty" is used in the opera's first romantic reference, by Ludwig to Lisa, and then recurs with reference to Ludwig's past perception of the now-disgusting sausage roll: "Through the repetition, sex is strongly identified with indigestion, and the rhyme both times with 'hasty' suggests premature ejaculation, or at any rate some kind of sexual dysfunction" (see 179–80). These intriguing readings of the last two high Savoy operas suggest that Gilbert's disinclination to exalt erotic union

eventually became so ingrained that it finally began to express itself (unconsciously, we presume) even in his seemingly innocuous word choices.
77. Phyllis Karr, "*Utopia* vs. *Ruddigore?*" *Gasbag* 13, no. 5 (1982): 20. See Stedman, "William S. Gilbert," 387, for a similar view.
78. Baily, *G + S Book*, 228.

III: Conclusion

1. For Frye's statements on the settings, conclusions, and structure of masque, see *Anatomy*, 288, 293, and 289 respectively.
2. Frye, *Anatomy*, 287–88; G. K. Chesterton, "Gilbert and Sullivan," in *The Eighteen-Eighties: Essays by Fellows of the Royal Society of Literature*, ed. Walter de la Mare (Cambridge: Cambridge Univ. Press, 1930); rpt. in *W. S. Gilbert: A Century of Scholarship*, 184.
3. Frye, *Anatomy*, 165; Sypher, Appendix, 242–44; Ellis, "Comic Vision," 71.
4. Perry, "Victorianism of W. S. Gilbert," 154–55.
5. Frye, *Anatomy*, 287; Wolfson, *Final Curtain*, 42, 42–43, 98; "The New Savoy Opera," rev. of *The Grand Duke*, *Sunday Times* 8 March 1896: 6.
6. Williamson, *Gilbert and Sullivan*, 14. For a similar view of the last two operas, see, e.g., Goldberg, *Story of G + S*, 415 and 428–29.
7. Altick, *Victorian People*, 295, 296–97; Harrold and Templeman, Introductory Survey, *English Prose*, lxxix.
8. George Rowell, Introduction to *The Second Mrs. Tanqueray*, *Late Victorian Plays: 1890–1914*, 2nd ed. (London: Oxford Univ. Press, 1972), 1–2; W. S. Gilbert, *Charity, Original Plays: First Series*, 106; [Kate Field], "W. S. Gilbert," *Scribner's Magazine* 18 (1879): 753.
9. Wilde's borrowings from *Engaged* have been noted by several critics: see, e.g., Lynton Hudson, *The English Stage, 1850–1950* (London: Harrap, 1950), 102–5.
10. See Rowell, *Victorian Theatre*, 134, 154.
11. Knight, *Golden Labyrinth*, 342–43.
12. Rowell, *Victorian Theatre*, 134.
13. Thorndike, *English Comedy*, 562.
14. See Rowell, *Victorian Theatre*, 129.
15. See Nicoll, *Late Nineteenth Century Drama*, 1:61.
16. Thorndike, *English Comedy*, 568.
17. See St. John Ervine, *Bernard Shaw: His Life, Work and Friends* (New York: Morrow, 1956), 304.
18. Sawyer, *Comedy of Manners*, 139.
19. George Bernard Shaw, "Gilbert and Solomon," rev. of *The Nautch Girl*, by George Dance and Edward Solomon, 8 July 1891, rpt. in *Gasbag* 12, no. 7 (1981): 20; Nicoll, *Late Nineteenth Century Drama*, 1:187–88; "Our Stage To-Day," *The Theatre* ns 24 (Sept. 1894): 89–96.
20. On the revivals of the nineties, see Allen, "Encore: The First Nights of the First Revivals," *First Night Gilbert and Sullivan*, 459–61.
21. Filon, *English Stage*, 153.
22. See Goodman, *Gilbert and Sullivan at Law*, 122.
23. Pearson, *Gilbert*, 77.
24. See Baily, *G + S Book*, 397.

25. Max Beerbohm, "Mr. Gilbert's Rentrée (and Mine)," rev. of *The Fairy's Dilemma*, by W. S. Gilbert, *Saturday Review* 14 May 1904; rpt. in *Around Theatres* (1924; New York: Taplinger, 1969), 326. Gilbert himself seems to have recognized the validity of Beerbohm's point: in a letter to the actress who played Angela, he admitted that "The piece came too late—it should have been produced forty years ago, and then people would have appreciated its intention" (Letter to Mrs. Arthur Bourchier, 2 August 1904, in Dark and Grey, *W. S. Gilbert*, 163).

Index